In Praise of Politics

In Praise of Politics

Alain Badiou
with Aude Lancelin

Translated by Susan Spitzer

polity

Polity Press
65 Bridge Street
Cambridge CB2 1UR, UK

Polity Press
101 Station Landing
Suite 300
Medford, MA 02155, USA

ISBN-13: 978-1-5095-3367-1 (hardback)
ISBN-13: 978-1-5095-3368-8 (paperback)

A catalogue record for this book is available from the British Library.

Library of Congress Cataloging-in-Publication Data

Names: Badiou, Alain, interviewee. | Lancelin, Aude, interviewer.
Title: In praise of politics / Alain Badiou, Aude Lancelin.
Other titles: Éloge de la politique. English
Description: English edition. | Medford, Massachusetts : Polity Press, [2019] | Includes bibliographical references and index.
Identifiers: LCCN 2018040026 (print) | LCCN 2018054194 (ebook) | ISBN 9781509533701 (Epub) | ISBN 9781509533671 | ISBN 9781509533671(Hardback) | ISBN 9781509533688(Paperback)
Subjects: LCSH: Political science--Philosophy. | Badiou, Alain--Interviews.
Classification: LCC JA71 (ebook) | LCC JA71 .B26413 2019 (print) | DDC 320.01--dc23
LC record available at https://lccn.loc.gov/2018040026

Typeset in 12.5 on 15 pt Adobe Garamond by
Servis Filmsetting Ltd, Stockport, Cheshire
Printed and bound in Great Britain by CPI Group (UK) Ltd, Croydon

For further information on Polity, visit our website:
politybooks.com

Contents

I

What Is Politics?

What a strange idea, we'll be told, to be coming out in praise of politics in the year of a presidential election [2017], when that election was distinguished above all by its exposure of a broken-down landscape ever more shockingly abandoned to the free play of the forces of capital. One really has to wonder what might still be of interest to a philosopher in such a case. How do you respond to people, young people in particular, who can't imagine politics as anything other than an arena for cynicism and opportunism?

That kind of feeling can only be understood by asking, first, what exactly is meant by the word "politics." It's a long story. From the beginning of the story, several millennia ago, the idea was that politics was power, the issue of the assumption and exercise of state power vis-à-vis established communities, communities whose members were known and identified. The first definition therefore considers that the central – indeed, sole – issue of politics is state power. It's a simple definition but one that nevertheless runs through all of history: it was still Lenin's definition, for example, and is still ours as well, in a rudimentary form, when politics is reduced to the electoral choice of a president.

This definition may give rise to a very cynical conception of politics as consisting of competition, rivalry, and ruthlessness, with the aim of seizing power, assuming it, and wielding it as one sees fit. There are theorists of politics so conceived, foremost among them being undoubtedly Machiavelli. Machiavelli described in an extremely sophisticated, positivistic, one might even say "technical," way the various methods of struggle for the seizure and assumption of power as well as the qualifications needed for engaging in that kind of fight. He occupies a unique position as a theorist of politics, if it is conceived in these terms. Admittedly, we see little else today than that fight, with all that entails in terms of baseness, corruption, deceit, violence, and so on. But then, the author of *The Prince* had already showed that these elements were strongly associated with the question of politics and its exercise.

In contrast to this vision there developed, over a very turbulent, complex history, and in close connection with philosophy, another conception of politics: one that holds that politics has a constitutive relationship with justice. Throughout their historical existence (admittedly not a very long one, about twenty centuries), philosophers have endeavored to give a precise definition of justice. But whatever the definition, if the idea of justice is involved in the definition of politics then it can no longer be defined simply as the struggle for power. The central question becomes: "What is a just power?" And the debate over politics is less about the exercise of power than about the norms to which power is subject, its relationship to the community, and its objectives.

Between politics defined as power – focused entirely on the power of the state – and politics defined as justice – focused on questions like "What of the community, the relationship among its members, its aspirations? What of categories like equality and freedom?" – there is both a connection and a conflict. There is a connection because, ultimately, justice cannot remain a purely abstract idea with no bearing on the reality of the state. So, the question of justice is also, necessarily, the question of a just *power*. And, on the other hand, there is a conflict, because power divorced from the concept of justice is subject to the degradations that have occurred throughout history and of which the 2017 presidential election in France is but one episode. And hardly a brilliant one, considering all the corruption and sinister developments it involved.

The conflict between justice and power itself has a long history. Plato had already attempted to establish the standards for a state governed by the idea of the Good and had shown, through a very sophisticated analysis of the different "types" of government – oligarchy, democracy, timocracy, and anarchy – that it was no easy task. Relatively late in the day, no doubt around the eighteenth century, with Rousseau in particular, and later through the efforts of such nineteenth-century revolutionary thinkers as Marx and Engels, of course, but also Proudhon, Fourier, and Feuerbach, not to mention Auguste Comte and Blanqui, the hypothesis that justice may actually be incompatible with power emerged. Consequently, the perspective on politics changed: state power might only be a transitory instrument, one that was necessary for a whole period of history but would be replaced by the establishment of a justice that would be, as it were, in the hands of humanity itself. This might be the dialectical movement that overcomes the opposition between justice and power.

Your philosophical system defines politics as a "truth procedure," along with love, art, and science. In what sense do you mean this? Certainly, there's a general belief that nothing could be further from politics than a concern for truth . . .

Sure, and as a matter of fact Machiavelli defined politics broadly as a sovereign art of lying. An ability to lie has always been considered a necessity for politicians in general, if only to win power by making promises that won't be kept. When I define politics as a "truth procedure," I obviously mean politics in the second sense we've just considered, namely when it is organically linked to the category of justice.

Is this an idealistic vision? I don't think so at all. I know – I had firsthand experience of this for many years – that politics is also, and perhaps above all, a practice, a process. It requires participants, activists, organizations, and popular movements, and all those things combined make for a very complex process, which yields the truth about what the community deserves to be, based on its political activity. Namely, a community no longer subject to arbitrary authorities or inexplicable divisions but a community, a collectivity, that is its own guide and provides its own direction, based on a shared standard of justice.

Whenever a novelty of this kind occurs in the political field, that is, whenever a new opportunity arises of doing away with an old, unjust, inegalitarian, and divided order in favor of an order that could be regarded as humanity's exerting of control over its own destiny – whenever something like that occurs, it's an innovation, a creation, in the domain of history. And that innovation has a very special destiny because it is an exception to the general regime: state administration and indifference to any idea of justice. It is well known that revolutions have always enthralled huge crowds precisely because they offered such novelty. Their historical destiny is another story. But the revolutions I have in mind, from the most egalitarian phase of the French Revolution (1792–4) to the Cultural Revolution in China (1965–70), by way of the revolution in Haiti led by Toussaint Louverture (1791–1802), the Paris Commune (1871), and the Russian Revolution (1917–29), have already demonstrated historically – and this is an irreversible, established fact – that collective ownership of justice is possible. This is what I call a truth. A truth of what? Of a human community's ability to take control of its own destiny and form of organization.

A moment ago, you mentioned a community that is its own guide, that takes control of its own destiny, as being the just system of government, the one we should strive for, the most desirable one. In our democracies, as everyone knows, the people's role is usually limited to choosing from among a handful of candidates and, once power has been handed over to one of them, the people disappear. More often than not, they even become nuisances and have to be told to let the grown-ups handle things. When they are *consulted, which is rarely the case, that decision is immediately regretted, and their input is usually ignored. So, I would simply ask you this question: in what sense are we still living in a democracy, in your opinion?*

We need to go back to the definition given that word today. Ever since the invention of the parliamentary system by the English in the late eighteenth century, democracy has been conceived of not as a real figure of collective life but as a form of the state. That the word "democracy" actually ultimately means only one form of state among others is something Plato had already remarked on, and so did Lenin. What is the defining feature of that form of the state? Its defining feature is that it presents itself *as a representation*: the representatives of the people, the elected officials, the members of legislative assemblies, are responsible for managing the affairs of the state.

In the eyes of this system's proponents, it operates "democratically" since the people are regularly consulted, and, after all, they are free to remove the leaders they don't like and elect ones they do. If that's all democracy is – the representative figure and the electoral organization of political life – then I'd say that we're living in a democracy, but I'd add . . . so much the worse for us. And so much the worse for democracy. There is obviously another conception of democracy that corresponds to its Greek etymology: *demos* (the people) / *kratos* (power). Rather than including the idea of representation, this "power of the people" makes it illegitimate. This issue has been debated for a long time: Rousseau, for example, who was one of the foremost theorists of democracy in the eighteenth century, thought that the English-type representative figure did not merit the name "democracy," that it wasn't democratic because it was the periodic designation of representatives who in actual fact did more or less whatever they felt like and lied through their teeth to the people.

In any case, if we use the word "democracy" we need to specify which meaning we're giving it: an electoral and representative system subordinated to state power, or actual processes that are the possible expression of a popular will on specific issues. The latter definition is clearly the operative one in certain circumstances. It emerges or has emerged, for example, in general assemblies during factory strikes or in the recent history of occupations of deliberative spaces in some countries. Large mass movements don't designate stable, electoral delegations. They decide on their ideological and practical orientation in various types of gatherings of the people themselves, and on their instruction – in small or mass meetings

– by speakers and leaders in whom people have confidence, a confidence justified by their experience, not by representative procedures.

I think that we know, that everyone knows, that the system we live in isn't democratic in the authentic sense of the word. Especially since – and this is important – we're not even sure that the people we vote for in the electoral ritual, who are supposed to represent us, are really the ones who decide what's going to happen in the real world. It seems obvious that there are masters whose power is far greater than that of our elected officials. The heads of multinational corporations, who are not elected by anyone and are accountable only to shareholders concerned solely with their financial gains, have far more influence with our governments than any popular assembly. The economic and financial issue today, even in the opinion of the elected leaders, no matter who they are, is so tough in terms of governance that not only do our representatives ultimately do nothing but represent, but most of the time they're only doing it for show. They have no real power when it comes to most of the important issues. What with international pressure, organizations like the European Commission that are accountable to no one, the heads of major corporations, the transnational power of the banks, the threat posed by agencies that determine countries' financial "rating," not to mention the military and other state administration bodies, an entire apparatus of power revolves around the state, stringently limits its freedom of action, and reduces the ordinary citizen's contribution to a pathetic summons, every four or five years, to take part in something that is just a charade of decisions that have already been made elsewhere.

Isn't the sense of democratic dispossession we feel an inevitable evil in countries as large as ours, though? You mentioned Rousseau a moment ago, and that happens to be one of his objections to the idea of mass democracy in The Social Contract. *He thought that true democracy could not exist other than in small communities, small countries, where the people could be consulted frequently and in a very direct way . . .*

Here we're getting into an examination of the political process conceived of not as periodic state-mandated appointments but as a thought-practice exercised by the people themselves for specific purposes. To my mind, that's what politics is about, first and foremost. I think we need to conceive of politics without immediately connecting it to the state. If we're completely fixated on the state, the first thing we'll say is: politics is about seizing control of the state, because if we don't seize control of the state we can't do anything, we have no power. But that's not true. Politics includes, for example, the crucial element that is the vision we have and uphold of what humanity, or at least the community to which we belong, should become. This community exists in the form of large countries, of course, but it also exists on a wide variety of scales. It is represented at the national level, at the town or village level, in large companies, in foreign worker hostels, and so on. So, society is actually a complex network, within which there is always the possibility of calling meetings and discussing what people want to do.

Who can do this? Who can organize such discussions, and the practical decisions that result from them, on every possible level? Obviously, the people with a strategic vision of what society should become. After all, in its practical reality, politics is a relationship formed between the people who have a pretty clear vision of society's future, on the one hand, and, on the other, the real and concrete existence of that society itself, at a particular level. This was what was called "mass work" during the "red years," from 1965 to 1975. The activist is someone who has an idea about the community's destiny; who in his or her own life explores new paths in society; who meets as many people living in different circumstances as possible; who discusses their circumstances with them; who helps to explain those circumstances from a global perspective; who engages in a simultaneous work of education, discussion, and clarification; who listens to the ideas of the people living in those circumstances; and who ultimately works with them to change those circumstances, on whatever level he or she happens to be. That level may very well be a market, a city, or in certain circumstances, a region or a country; it depends on the circumstances, which are circumstances of history.

The intersection of politics and history is a major issue. Politics only becomes historical, strictly speaking, in exceptional circumstances, during what I would call political events, events that create unprecedented opportunities for people on a large scale. This was certainly the case with the advent of democracy in Athens, with significant reformers like Solon or Cleisthenes, amid tremendous unrest linked to the agrarian problem. Another example is the extraordinarily turbulent period of civil wars in England, between the seventeenth and eighteenth centuries, from which the invention of the parliamentary system of government ultimately emerged. I could also mention what the great popular uprisings of 1936 meant to my father, or what the totally unexpected May 1968 meant to me. Or, to take a more recent example, consider the massive, sustained protests of "the Arab Spring." But even if opportunities like these don't exist in a given situation, well, we'll just have to work on a smaller scale then. There has to be political conviction, and we know that if it exists on a small scale, that will greatly boost its existence on a large scale when an event seizes and mobilizes a large part of the population. What I think is that politics comes down to making an idea exist in a given situation. To "be involved in" politics, you not only need to have a sound vision based on a general discussion of what the community can and should become, but you also need to try out that idea, that vision, on whatever level you can.

A major political event, in my opinion, is the

moment when that possibility begins to exist on a large scale. That's when the people who will express their views, steer the course of events, and make decisions emerge from all the places where there had been small-scale discussions and initiatives. The state should not necessarily be regarded as something that must absolutely be taken over. However, if in a context like this the state strongly and vigorously opposes the flourishing of such democracy, which is the *real* kind of democracy, then the necessary conclusions will have to be drawn from that. Fight it? Retreat? Wait and see? These are decisions that depend on the situation itself.

At this point, we need to initiate a more intense discussion. Indeed, I think that in the contemporary world – and probably since the French Revolution, in fact – there are two basic orientations, or let's say two alternatives, and only two, at the level that I call the Idea. And I think that politics is ultimately the conflictual dialectic between these two sole orientations, where they both exist.

On the one hand, there's the dominant orientation – overwhelmingly dominant, alas, today – whereby the true masters of societies are, inevitably, the masters of the economy, that is, the owners of the means of production and other such gatekeepers of the financial sphere. This alternative implies that, to a large extent, political alternation doesn't matter: in the end, the various elected leaders will all do pretty much the same thing, because that's what a free-market economy requires. This alternative can be fairly and simply called "the capitalist way." That's been its name for the past two centuries.

And then there is – minimally, or barely, or there was once more forcefully – another alternative. It holds that the community must take back all its means of existence and that it must especially take back all the economic, productive, and financial means. This is the alternative that used to be called "the communist way." Not only do I think that we should continue to call it that but giving up the term would be tantamount to accepting defeat. That term, understood in its original sense, says exactly what should be said. Indeed, the alternative I'm talking about involves putting things in common and placing ourselves under the imperative of the common good. If that is the case, then politics in no way consists in choosing the best managers of contemporary capitalism's health. It is the putting into practice of the conviction that what is common, the common good, should, in effect, be enjoyed in common.

The existence of these two alternatives, the capitalist one and the communist one, is the key principle underlying the actual existence of political discussion. If the discussion of the analyses and decisions among the people – in meetings, demonstrations, and rallies – fails to take place in the context of a struggle between the two alternatives, then it will inevitably turn into a purely managerial and ultimately apolitical discussion.

The candidates who ran in the last election all proposed slightly different ways of managing existing capitalism, but that's all. Some said the rules should be tightened, while others said they should be relaxed, but they all agreed that it was ultimately a matter of administering the existing system of capitalist domination, regarded as inescapable.

In my view, the conflation of administration and politics today is totally disastrous for politics. Politics begins when there are two main orientations, two alternative paths, and when, most of all, the choice is about the path we are taking and how it can and must exist in the situation, at every level.

Does that mean that, in your view, between what's known as "the right" and communism there is nothing, no political hypothesis, that can really be taken seriously?

Between the communist orientation and the right, there's the left. The non-communist left, at least in Europe, has in practice meant, in terms of the facts and the practical realities of state power – in other words, for most of its history, from its inception in the latter half of the nineteenth century – socialist or social-democratic parties. Can you deny that those parties are responsible for the biggest disappointments we've ever experienced? Let's not forget that the newly emerging left, which claimed to be republican, radical, and socialist – the left of Jules Ferry, Jules Favre, Gambetta, and Jules Guesde, but also that of Bernstein and Kautsky and Noske in Germany – overwhelmingly supported the crushing of the Paris Commune, the worst kind of colonialism, and ultimately the chauvinistic frenzy that led to the bloodbath of World War I. I got my political education during the Algerian War, under a socialist government that significantly increased the war's inconceivable brutality. And what about the whole sorry scam that the Mitterrand escapade turned out to be from 1983 on? Or the liberal "reforms" of Schröder in Germany, the most notable effect of which was that 30 percent of the population in that country, whose economic exploits are vaunted by our ruling caste, was reduced to extreme poverty?

Believe me, what I've learned from history and my own personal experience makes me tempted to quote Aragon: "Fire on the trained bears of social democracy!"

But still, historical socialism, the real one, the socialism of a Pierre Leroux or a Jean Jaurès (I'm obviously not talking about Solférinian socialism,[1] which recently expired), or even anarchism, the anarchism of a Proudhon or a Bakunin, are leftwing traditions that exist, after all. They have no merit as far as you're concerned?

OK, there are some exceptions, but ultimately very few. Rosa Luxemburg and Karl Liebknecht

1 The Paris headquarters of the Socialist Party are located on the rue de Solférino, hence "Solférinian socialism," which, as Lancelin remarks, had virtually imploded after the 2017 elections, if not before.

were without a doubt great figures of social democracy. But look at what happened to them: they led a defeated uprising, which was actually inspired far more by communism than socialism, and they were murdered, on the orders of a socialist minister. You mentioned Jaurès: he was a very decent man, thanks in particular to his anti-war stance, his support for miners' strikes, and his justifiable suspicion of colonial expeditions. But did he represent a real political movement, a "hypothesis" forged in real popular processes? He was primarily a great parliamentary orator, with no real influence over the government's actions. He embodied that simultaneously necessary and useless attribute of our "democracies": the opposition. Because "opposition" implies that you actually agree with the majority on the rules of the political game and that you'll peacefully make way for your worst enemies. And to return to Jaurès, look at what happened to him, too.[2]

Actually, there has always been a left wing of the left, usually located within a socialist party or behind some small parties or organizations.

2 Jaurès was assassinated in July 1914, on the eve of World War I, by a nationalist fanatic.

That's where I myself come from: I started out in the SFIO [the French Section of the Workers' International] and, as a result of our complete disagreement with the party leadership regarding the Algerian War, I took an active part in the "far-left" split that eventually led to the creation of the PSU [the Unified Socialist Party]. I'll grant you that some of the organized forces and practices of a vibrant communism often emerge, on the left, from deep within mediocre social democracy. Even Lenin and the Bolsheviks, even Rosa Luxemburg and the Spartacists, came from schisms within a "big," blatantly opportunistic socialist party. But that's precisely the proof that political vitality can only ever exist, in the established left, as something that breaks away, often violently, from that left. For the most part, the left has always been an institution of the dominant power; it's one variation of it. At best, the left is the womb from which a newborn baby of communism at times emerges.

Anarchism is a different matter. Bakunin and Marx were in agreement on any number of things when they created the First International together, not least the idea of the end of the state. And there are any number of issues that need to be analyzed and discussed regarding the way the Catalan anarchists attempted a radical reorganization of their province during the Spanish Civil War. What I believe is that anarchy is an ideology of the movement, a creative negativity, but it's never a politics per se. There's a festive, existential dimension to anarchism that often conceals a brutal kind of intolerance and only feels comfortable in intermittent activism.

Finally, if the question of the present is capitalism and its demise, the new politics can only be some form of communism. It opposes, or will oppose, the contemporary consensus that politics is at best the most rational administration possible of an eternal capitalism.

2

The Communist Hypothesis

Since the fall of the Berlin Wall, and actually even since the late 1970s, only one alternative seems to be accepted in the West when it comes to politics: managerial politics, run by the people Marx called "the agents of capital" and from which communist politics would seem to be totally shut out, even excluded from the real discussion. The governmental lefts no longer even "try" – in Europe as a whole – to make people believe they represent a different alternative. All the so-called socialist parties have by now embraced the neoliberal order, and even the so-called radical-left parties are more like splinter groups of that pseudo-socialism and don't correspond to the communist idea as you'd like to revive it. So, I would simply ask you this question, even if it's fraught with difficulties: how can we reopen that particular possibility, given that the word itself has been banished from politics?

When a key word like "communism" has been banished from politics, there's nothing to do, to begin with, but try to bring it back. That in itself is a crucial struggle. We've got to overcome, everywhere, the fear that the word triggers, people's ignorance about what it means, and never consent, for the sake of expediency, to its being eliminated. Many people have advised me to stop using the word, to replace it with a different one. But it's perfectly clear today that the elimination of the word is nothing less than the elimination of the alternative it used to refer to, and therefore the shameful acceptance of the total hegemony of the other alternative, the capitalist way.

We should first ask where the fatal sabotage of everything the word "communism" once meant, and still means, comes from. Why did the communist hypothesis, which had been extremely strong right from its inception in the 1840s, disappear so suddenly? This alternative had been conceived of, in Marx's *Communist Manifesto*, as a new way of looking at human history as a whole. All worker uprisings and peasant insurrections since then have been based on it. All victorious revolutions have derived their meaning from it. It has achieved considerable successes, which changed the course of history in the twentieth century in countries as important as Russia and China and as determined and courageous as Yugoslavia and Cuba. And, given all this, they want us to dump the word "communism"?

You see, I think that an important task, a task of thought, is first and foremost to *make an independent assessment of this*, that is, not to go along with the dominant assessment of the communist experiments, an assessment that's obviously deeply flawed and self-serving and is a key element in the ostensible "triumph" of contemporary liberalism.

The dominant assessment is basically that it was all – "as we now know" – criminal. So, it's not even worth talking about it or debating it anymore: the case is closed, everyone agrees, no one likes crime.

Basically, that's not just an attempt to defeat an orientation in the ideological-political field but an attempt to do away with it altogether. And it all dates from the 1980s; it's fairly recent. I think the great victory of the capitalist reaction in the latter part of the twentieth century, right after the big upheavals of the 1960s and 1970s, consisted in eliminating the alternative hypothesis, in making it seem as though it no longer existed.

In criminalizing it essentially . . .

Right, by using every means necessary to ensure that public opinion was completely clueless when it came to this issue. So, to begin with, there's a very important task, which is to make our own assessment of the failure of historical communism, of the failure of the "socialist states," *based on retaining the hypothesis, not on eliminating it.* On the basis of this hypothesis, on the basis of the communist alternative to which we're committed, we need to explain why the various "socialist states" collapsed, and why, to revive politics, we've got to get past that failure. This is a very fine but important distinction. We shouldn't repeat the explanations that have been given by the dominant criminalization but rather ask the question this way: How is it that, even though the explicit objective of this emancipatory political alternative was to gradually undermine the independence and authority of the state, it instead resulted in extremely brutal, concentrated, authoritarian states? And we also need to ask why, even though the communist agenda has always been about combatting what it called the "great differences," that is, the difference between intellectual and manual labor, between city and countryside, and between management tasks and implementation tasks, nothing like that happened, except for the exciting proposals of the final phase (1971–5) of the Cultural Revolution in China. One of the basic objectives of communism in all its forms was to propose an idea of labor that Marx called the idea of the polymorphous worker: society would no longer be divided into specialized and, of course, always hierarchized, categories, the most menial jobs being the lowest-paid ones and management tasks being highly compensated. How did it happen that, instead, such specialization, particularly in the Soviet Union, became set in stone?

Incidentally, I'd like to highlight the efforts undertaken in that direction in China, despite the ultimate failure that Deng Xiaoping's 1976 coup d'état represented. We can, and should, read the admirable texts, particularly the ones produced by workers from the Shanghai Machine-Tool Factory, who explained how they'd tried to ensure that factory management would be completely different from factory management in the West, where the capitalist law of productivity is imposed on the workers, who are renamed "the workforce"; how you could collect the workers' suggestions for improving the organization of work and do something with them; how there should be discussions between management and the workers about the initiatives, even the technical initiatives. There was a tremendous ferment of ideas, and that's the sort of thing we should draw on to uphold the principles of communism. Because, in actual fact, it's not because they were communist that the "socialist states" failed but because they weren't communist *enough* and didn't maintain the political tension, the constant discussion – in a word, the struggle between the two alternatives – in the collective life of the people, with regard to all the critical practical issues involving the principles of communism.

Could you just remind us what you consider to be the main principles of communism?

There are four main principles of communism. They can be listed very simply.

The first principle is to wrest control of the

means of production from private ownership. The capitalist oligarchy currently dominating the whole world must be done away with. One statistic that I constantly repeat, because it's important to be aware of it, is that, today, 260 people possess as much, in terms of income and wealth, as three billion other people, which is a *phenomenal* concentration of wealth, without precedent in human history. That has got to stop. That's the first principle.

The second principle is to try to do away with the specialized division of labor, in particular the hierarchical divisions between management tasks and implementation tasks and, more generally, between intellectual and manual labor.

The third principle is to try to put an end to the obsession with identities and in particular with national identity. Let's not forget that, among other things, Marx said, with a certain vehemence, that "the workers have no country." So, let's stop imprisoning politics in a straitjacket of identities, be they racial, national, religious, sexual, or other. That is also a basic objective.

And the last main principle, which in a way underpins all the others, is to do all this not by constantly strengthening the authoritarian mechanisms of the state but, on the contrary, by gradually diluting the state in collective deliberations, something Marx called "the withering away of the state," to make way, he said, for "free association."

So, to answer your question, the failure of what can be called the state communisms of the previous period, or the period of "socialist states," should be examined in relation to these four principles. To what extent did they really try to implement them? To what extent, on the contrary, did they try to bypass them for the sake of economic development and power? The idea being to locate the roots of this historical communism's failure in an *unfaithfulness* to itself rather than, as is commonly claimed, in a stubborn faithfulness to itself. It was by being unfaithful to itself, that is, by dividing, by creating a conservative oligarchy within itself, that this communism eventually failed. An obvious example of this is the fact that China, which has become a major imperial and capitalist power today, didn't even need to change the name of its dominant party, the Chinese Communist Party, which clearly has absolutely nothing communist about it, isn't communist in the least. But if the party has been able to continue calling itself that, it proves that there was a gradual abandonment of the objectives of the original politics of emancipation within the dominant political party itself. An abandonment of communism, under the name of "communism."

But how do you respond to the people – and there are an awful lot of them – who think that the failure of communism was inscribed in the very nature of its project and that, as it went so determinedly against the way of the world, communism could only operate by using the utmost violence? How do you counter the idea that "to change man" is in itself a promise fraught with danger?

That man, the human animal, corresponds to the description given of him by dominant capitalism is a completely erroneous anthropological hypothesis. The basic idea behind all this, which in fact underpins the subservience of politics to dominant economic interests, is that man is a nasty animal, reducible to a caricature of the "struggle for life" borrowed – mistakenly – from Darwin. People are allegedly necessarily self-interested, individuals are driven only by the principles of their own power and survival, competition is the driving force behind innovation, and so on.

The truth is, there are countless examples to the contrary. Of course, selfless action often appears as a struggle or a conflict with the powers that have made self-interest and money their sole criterion. Under the conditions of dominant capitalism, this conflict may even occur within the same person, in the guise of an inner split or an inability to decide. But even under these conditions, the idea that self-interest is the absolute center of human existence, whether individual or collective, is quite simply wrong, in my opinion. I'm not saying, of course, that there's no such thing as self-interest, but there are countless examples of people passionately doing things that are dictated not by their own self-interest but by the interest of others, of the community, of the people they know, by the interest of the group they belong to, and who thus naturally go beyond their private interests in their long-term and day-to-day activities.

In a way, capitalism requires people to sacrifice themselves for an "ethics" of private interest, which is a most terrible paradox. People are told: "We are well aware that what you like is being rich; so, to make sure you get rich, start by becoming a little poorer: work hard." This is a vision of humanity that there's no reason to accept.

In fact, opposing positions on the subject had developed as early as the eighteenth century. It is ultimately the Hobbes versus Rousseau debate, which we're still having. For Hobbes, man is a wild animal who must be tamed by external forces, while for Rousseau, man is good, naturally good. "Naturally good": what does that mean? It simply means that the human animal has resources and capabilities that enable it to act for motives that go beyond the immediate conception of its own self-interest. In other words, it's not exactly an animal. And *I* think that the capitalist vision of humanity is that humanity, as I said, is a nasty animal species and it must therefore be subjected to . . . what? To a system of organized interests that will ultimately lead to the luckiest people, the people with the most advantages, the people with inherited wealth, winning, and everyone else being losers.

I don't think you can completely reduce every vision that's different from communism to the most narrow-minded

> *capitalism, in which man is only driven by an extremely limited sense of his own self-interest. Communism doesn't conflict with just that one vision of man. In fact, for Rousseau himself, man is by no means a selfless being, strictly speaking. On the contrary, he is completely driven by "self-love"* [l'amour de soi], *and the interest he may take in other people is an extension of this self-love, which depends on the feeling that might be aroused in him by another sensitive being in whom he recognizes himself. For Hume, too, man is neither wholly dominated by self-interest nor is he selfless. He is simply described as someone who is "partial," that is, not everything he does is driven by self-interest in the narrowest sense of the term; it can sometimes be driven by the interest he takes in certain people around him or by concern for a certain number of things that matter to him. So, is the debate about the communist idea really between narrow self-interest, on the one hand, and all-round altruism, on the other?*

I think that, as far as actual politics is concerned, that *is* in fact the case. We shouldn't forget that capitalism's only rule is profit. The dictatorship of profit in capitalism is thus involved even in the organization of production and society itself. And it greatly increases the need for this dictatorship to have an overall vision of humanity that's directly related to profit and task specialization and that eliminates all protest based on the idea of justice or equality. That's the problem.

At the time of the debate among Rousseau, Hobbes, and Hume, a tiny oligarchy did not yet own half of humanity's wealth; the planetary hegemony of big capital did not yet exist. Where these thinkers were concerned, the most powerful owner was the landowner, the local aristocrat, and it was in that historical context that they discussed the subjective position of profit-sharing. They were tempted, of course, to promote "the mean value," i.e., the small landowner, who naturally cared about the profitability of his property but was reasonably generous. He was, moreover, the main ideological hero of the French Revolution. But in contemporary capitalism that "hero" has become a loser. In no way are sharing and moderation the basic law of capitalism. Its cult of self-interest is rampant because the (scientific) law of capitalist development is capital concentration. And we see spectacular examples of this every day. You yourself, by being summarily fired, paid the price for the fact that your conception of journalism didn't concur with that of the triumvirate of big capitalists who bought your magazine, *L'Obs*, which can now be called *L'Obscène*. The only thing your former bosses care about is their own self-interest. They're proud of the fact, moreover, and are pleased as punch with their view of things. Most of the press and media in France have been bought up by the giants of the CAC 40 [the French equivalent of the Dow Jones Industrial Average]. And the same trend is going on in every sector.

The concentration of capital is so intense today that its ability to provide all of humanity with means of survival is questionable. This, by the way, was also one of Marx's predictions. The accumulation of capital may occur in such a way that, at some point, it would become impossible to make a profit if everyone were put to work. Today, there are probably three billion people who are neither wage earners nor owners of capital nor farmers with a plot of land, and they roam the world in search of a livelihood. In such a world, how can there be room for anything other than a clear-cut opposition between two alternative ways of life? How can the fundamental debate between capitalism and communism be avoided?

I of course fully agree with you that it's important to be nuanced, that any figure of subjectivity is dialectical. It is also the purpose of political discussions to recognize that there are disagreements over all the issues having to do with the common good, since the definition of the common good is always complicated. But today's world, particularly now that the masters of capital believe they're free from any other alternative and think the communist way is dead and buried, is a world of utter ferocity.

And let me add that, since it is still characterized by deep-seated rivalries, especially between the former dominant powers of the European and American West and the new capitalisms that have emerged from communism, namely the Russian and Chinese ones, it's a world that, if left to its own devices, will lead us into war, as it has already done twice during the past century. That's for sure.

OK, but the collectivization of the means of production wasn't exactly a resounding success in economic and human terms, and let's not even get started on the abolition of private property wherever it was implemented in the world at the time of the "actually existing" socialist

> *states. How should one answer, let me ask once again, those who think that this idea, the communist idea, whatever its intrinsic value, can only be translated into reality through violence?*

Again, that's really the criticism waged by liberal ideology, which views inequality and competition as the only real driving forces behind human action. I think we need to respond to it with arguments at different levels. We should begin by reminding people that, up to the 1970s, the USSR was clearly the second-largest world power. That socialist state, with its centralized economy, amazed the world, first by defeating the Nazi war machine, even in victorious, highly technical tank battles, then by being the first country to launch the space adventure. Next, it should be pointed out that there were spectacularly successful achievements made by certain types of non-competitive, monopolistic organizations in the immediate post-war period. For example, the electrification of the whole of France after 1945 was achieved under a state monopoly. At the time, nobody objected that there were fundamental flaws in the system. Not in the least! And it was a tremendous success. Renault, which was a non-competitive state-owned company back then, was an undeniable success, especially with its introduction of affordable "people's" vehicles – to such an extent that the Renault 4CV became the symbol of the "people's car." So, I think that, even on the level of economic production, the superiority of the competitive system has by no means been proven. It's an ideological myth.

Other political systems that are anything but altruistic and universally cooperative can achieve the same thing . . . Take Volkswagen, for example, which grew out of Hitler's desire in the 1930s to provide every German household with a car.

Of course! But what I'm saying with this example is simply that the currently dominant view that production only works under the competitive conditions imposed by the global market is a misconception. It's quite simply wrong, and it's intended to force all types of production to fit the dominant mold of the globalized capitalist economy. I just wanted to clarify that first point. Now for my second point, which I alluded to a moment ago but need to come back to: if the problem has to do with human nature, I would argue that there is no evidence that human nature is geared toward the privatization of everything rather than toward a conception of the public management of everything.

First, let's be clear: if by "private property" we mean possessing things needed for survival and personal development, it would be absurd to call for its abolition! What we're talking about here is private ownership of the means of production and exchange. Marx had already made it clear that he was not talking about private property in general but about *bourgeois* property. I have absolutely no doubt that such property could be abolished. It is quite clear that, after the expropriation and subsequent collectivization of their workplace, the dedication and even the excitement of workers, employees, all involved in both the management and the material process of production, can be relied on. There are myriad examples of dedication, generosity, and selflessness in the history of the human species, and I can't see why anyone would declare that these aspects of generosity and selflessness can't be encouraged so that they become dominant and contribute to the strength of a collectivized economy. I can't see why we should instead accept, encourage, and organize things in such a way that brute competition is dominant. In other words, competition is dominant only because the ideology of competition is dominant. If the ideology were no longer that one, if it were reversed, if the values of solidarity, dedication, and equality were cultivated a little more systematically, we'd realize that they constitute a human resource that is largely as effective as the focus on private interest.

Naturally, there will always be a conflict between the two alternative ways of life. There will always be circumstances where selfishness, the desire for domination, and the cult of private interest will prevail. I'm not elaborating some warm and fuzzy vision of human beings here. Every subjectivity is divided and self-contradictory, but the properly political question is which term of that contradiction we support. The systematic encouragement given to competition, to the desire to be a winner, to contempt for losers? That's the liberal ideology; there's no getting around it! And that liberal ideology must be fought with political means.

The truth is, countless human actions, including those praised today by the very people who advocate competition and selfishness, testify to the fact that the subjective resources on which the new communist politics is to be based do in fact exist to a large degree. For example, everyone has to acknowledge that the people who embodied reason and valor during the last war were the Resistance fighters, who were exposed to tremendous risks, and not the collaborators. Yet it was the opportunists, the collaborators, who were on the side of instant success and victorious competition! The idea of the subjective primacy of selfishness is not only wrong but extremely dangerous because its impact depends on the circumstances: in certain circumstances it may become a criminal idea, pure and simple. If the absolute law is really the law of competition and dominance over others, in a fascist-type political regime it will naturally also be tempting to get in good with the people in power! And indeed, most of the French CEOs of capitalist companies were in good with the people in power, with Pétain. That's why their companies could be nationalized at the Liberation.

Again, let me be clear, I really don't think that the communist idea only conflicts with a liberal, competitive view of human nature. Take the Christian idea, which was the first to assert the oneness of humanity, to consider the existing hierarchies null and void, to aim to morally rearm the weak against the injustice of the powerful: well, that idea, which was unacceptable to the political regimes of the time, didn't conflict with the liberal world view. The forces with which that profoundly anti-natural Christian ideology conflicted were the established forces of domination, which significantly predated the capitalist world view. The profoundly inegalitarian nature of human relations predates the liberal or neo-liberal period by quite some time – we can agree on that, can't we?

Of course we can! I'm in no way underestimating the enormous obstacles the new communism has to face, but I think it's always important to understand that the problem of human nature, as such, cannot be analyzed apart from what fosters one belief or another in a given social world. Even the Church failed in its attempt, as is well known. Why? Because where its official institutions were concerned, it accepted inequality. True, it had some amazing preachers; it had mendicant friars; it had Saint Francis of Assisi; it had all of that. In fact, if the Church is still remembered it's because of those things. It's surely not because of the Inquisition. But the fact is, from the time of the Emperor Constantine, thus very early on, it had agreed to become an official religion, an ideological machine within the state. We're talking about politics here: the main path taken by the churches, without exception, was to make a pact with the states and hence with the ruling classes who "held" these states. That's why nothing corresponding to a "communist" orientation, even in a very vague sense, could come out of the Church, apart from a few special cases, from Saint Francis of Assisi to the worker priests of the 1950s.

However, let's get back to your question. I also think that the established order has thus far always been inegalitarian, and that that's what's called the Neolithic Age. We don't know much about what came before it. There were little groups of hunters. But the so-called "Neolithic Revolution," for the first time, formed societies based on inequality, based entirely on the organization and conservation, by force when necessary, of significant inequalities. In all societies, for the past four thousand years, a ruling group, ruling unequally, on the basis on how much private property it owned, ran society, protected itself with a proper state apparatus, competed with other groups of the same type, and so on. We're still completely stuck in this situation. Capitalism is part of Neolithic culture. That's why Marx thought it was still prehistoric in nature. And so, of course, it can always be argued that that's the way things have been for thousands of years. It's true! That's the way things have been for thousands of years, and that's why communism is not a simple matter of storming the Winter Palace. Naturally, the Winter Palace has to be stormed, but even if you do storm it you'll still be in the Neolithic Age because the very concept of "palace" is a Neolithic concept.

That's why I was simply asking you: is there a human resource that can work constructively toward becoming dominant beyond the unequal framework that has been in place for thousands of years? A resource for a post-Neolithic political subjectivity? Well, I think there's no reason for the answer to be negative, because when you accept the negative answer, you're just accepting the fact that all known societies, ever since private property and the state that protects it have been in existence, have been inegalitarian and have fostered an inegalitarian view of human relations. And so, over the long run, this fostering of inequality has shaped our subjectivities. When you've been raised with the idea that it's better to be first in class rather than last, to be very rich rather than poor, and so on – and we've all been raised that way – well, it leaves its mark. But in exceptional circumstances you realize that the opposite tendency also exists and that when it manifests itself, it mobilizes considerable affect in you, as well as a new way of thinking. And it is this affect, this new way of thinking, that must be organized, structured, and sustained by the communist hypothesis. I absolutely believe that most people know such a thing exists within them, as a positive potentiality. I myself know from experience that when this potentiality is realized, it surpasses in zest and joy anything the old self-centered subjective organization has to offer.

So, I agree with you: it's a lengthy business because it involves nothing less than getting out of the Neolithic Age! But we shouldn't counter this with the idea of a sort of bare human nature that's doomed to unfair competition, because, in a way, that would be to view the human species as an animal species. Yet, in spite of everything, as long as the human species is capable of something that is its own unique achievement, something that no other living creature can do – in any field, for that matter – that capacity cannot be reduced to that of an animal.

It is wrong to claim that every society must be hierarchical, disciplined, militarized, and so on. That's one possible form of association, but it's an unnatural one. Let's be Marxist about this: we shouldn't underestimate the fact that it is existing circumstances that shape our consciousness rather than our consciousness that shapes existing circumstances. Our minds have been shaped by the idea of inequality and competition ever since the time of the pharaohs and the Chinese emperors. The communist idea was the first one to rebel against that model, after what was actually a very short and largely misguided preparatory phase of Christianity. In a certain way, Stalinism was a repetition of something similar to Catholicism: the statization of the communist idea, conceived of as the only path to its victory, was carried out in an authoritarian and violent way. But we have to put an end to that.

3

Revolutions Put to the Test of History

One of the obstacles to the return of the communist hypothesis that you are calling for is obviously also – as you mentioned earlier – the sheer magnitude of the crimes committed in its name in the twentieth century. This is hardly news to you, since you're always being criticized in the public arena by media intellectuals and other such journalist types – it's no secret – for persisting in what they *describe as an error,* perseverare diabolicum, *and for never having given up on defending not only the communist idea, from a theoretical point of view, but also some of its more recent, and more shameful, historical instances. I'm thinking, for example, of the Chinese Cultural Revolution, which you continue to largely defend. So, what I'd like to ask you is this: What lessons have you yourself learned from the enormous*

> *crimes committed in the name of communism? Because you* have *learned some, contrary to what some people say.*

That question is all the more legitimate in that I said earlier that we absolutely must propose our own assessment of "actually existing" communism as a whole. You see, I think that, central to the reflection on this issue, there's the question of the state, that is, the question we started with way back at the beginning of this discussion. Both before and during the 1917 revolution, Lenin still believed that power was the central question of politics. He would qualify that judgment later, in the 1920s. I think that, in the twentieth century, the figure of historical communism in a way boiled down to the deep conviction that if the state were under the control of an organization whose agenda was not capitalism but an economy of a different type, then the essential problem of the communist alternative would have been resolved. But that's incorrect, for a number of reasons.

The first is that oversight of the communist alternative, deliberation about the conditions of its existence and its future, cannot be delegated, cannot be subject to the law of representation. In other words, the idea of the party of the proletariat, or the communist party, as concentrating in itself the entire political process is mistaken. We now know that it's wrong. Yet it was a very popular idea, and that's understandable because it's clear that the Russian Revolution was in a sense an event unprecedented in history. It was the first time that people came to power not because they were representatives of a particular sector of private ownership, whether agrarian or industrial, but simply because of the triumphant new force of the ideas they were defending and because of types of organization that helped them ensure that these ideas would be adopted by very broad swaths of public opinion. They came to power with brand-new tasks for which the simple party apparatus was insufficient because, on its own, it didn't represent enough control, by the people themselves, over their society's destiny – which was the basic agenda of communism, after all. And both Lenin and Mao Zedong (we really need to be acquainted with the texts) very quickly expressed concern about this issue. One of the last ideas of Lenin – who, in assessing the situation, said quite bluntly that, in the end, a clique of worthless state bureaucrats had been restored – was to set up what he called a workers' and peasants' inspectorate that would directly oversee the state. He wanted to move toward communism by calling on workers and peasants to form assemblies in which the state would be monitored. And Mao Zedong, whose constant line this was, launched the largest mass movement of the twentieth century, the Cultural Revolution, which incited tens of millions of young people, students, and workers to take to the streets in the cities. Who did he launch this movement against? Against the party-state, against the fusion of the state and the party. Mao was once asked: "You say the bourgeoisie is there, but where is this bourgeoisie?" He replied: "The bourgeoisie is in the Communist Party." He dialecticized the situation to the point where the mass movement ended up showing that the fusion of an extremely violent and authoritarian state with an all-powerful communist party was a deviation even as regards the communist movement. Because, in the final analysis, including under the principles of the communist alternative, it is the masses who make history.

The main lesson to be learned from all this

concerns politics specifically. Politics is not a simple matter of an organization with the ability to seize power taking control of a popular movement. Politics combines several different terms that must constantly be in a dialectical relationship with one another. One of them is the existence of real popular movements. The revolution that has brought new forces to power must not be the last mass movement, absolutely not. The masses must continue to be involved. As Mao said when speaking before millions of young people twenty years after the Chinese Communist Party seized power: "Get involved in state affairs."

I'd like to point out that people got very intensely involved in state affairs there, that even the government ministries were open to the masses, who entered the buildings, consulted the archives, and so on. Nothing like that had ever been seen anywhere else. This is an absolutely fundamental point: there must be popular movements. These movements will, as always, divide and disagree when put to the test of politics, but they must exist, especially when an issue is uncertain, unclear. People must be able to rebel, as Mao put it in a famous saying: "It is right to rebel against reactionaries." That's the first point.

The second point is that something will of course remain of state power for a long time to come. Hence the repeatedly proven risk of a sterile confrontation between the masses and the state. An intermediary organization is needed, that's for sure. Such an organization is necessary to organize politics over time, but it shouldn't merge with the state the way the Communist Party did. It should act as an intermediary, over time, over the long term, between what emerges from the popular movements, on the one hand, and the directives of the state, on the other. The problem, then, is a new dialectical relationship of politics as a whole, a dialectical relationship having not just two terms (the masses, on the one hand, and the state merging with the party, on the other) but three clearly distinct terms: the popular movement, which must be allowed the freedom to rebel or suggest new things; the organization, which must not merge with the state but must clarify and centralize what is being debated among the popular masses; and finally state power, which must be controlled as much as possible by the overall movement. This is what will have to be done in the centuries ahead, under the aegis of the third stage of communism, after Marx and Engels, and after Lenin and Mao as well: applying everywhere, as far as the political organization is concerned, something that Mao once said to Malraux: "We will give back to the masses in a clear form what they have given us in a confused form."

I remember seeing you, Slavoj Žižek, and Toni Negri in 2009 at an international conference to revive the word "communism." It was very striking to see that the auditorium at the Birkbeck Institute in London (which is not really known for being a world capital of Marxism) was full of young people, so many of them. What's happening with that revival today? Do you think the specter is on the prowl again, at least in people's minds?

I think that, as was the case between 1840 and 1860, there are two separate but interrelated tasks. The first is a sort of theoretical task in a broad sense: we need to bring the communist hypothesis back up to the surface, to put politics back into the question of the two alternatives. We've got to get back to a situation where there are two alternatives, not just one. That's a task that can also be accomplished in discussions with people, in demonstrations, wherever there are mobilizations, and so on. It's a huge subject of discussion because, as I mentioned, the assumption that there's only one alternative has been pervasive since the 1980s. Unless we can create a significant difference in the way people, on a large scale, think about just this one issue – the fact that we've got to move from the "one" to the "two" – we'll be in big trouble. Because even the large popular movements are confused by the absence of dual alternatives. They're trying to exist in a hostile environment, an environment where there's one dominant alternative, which claims to be the only possible one.

Have you felt that kind of uncertainty in the recent public squares movements?

Absolutely, even in the formidable, spectacular form of one of the largest of them, the Egyptian movement. It came together around the slogan "Mubarak, get out!", or, in other words, "Let's get rid of the military dictatorship," and it ended two years later with the pure and simple restoration of the military dictatorship. So, we need to think: Why was there this terrible backlash? Precisely because, in a way, the movement couldn't get beyond the assumption that there is only one alternative. After quite a long time, given that situation, pragmatism prevailed. In the absence of any direction, they chose from among the people who were there, who were part of the sole alternative: the Muslim Brotherhood first, and then General el-Sisi, a Mubarak clone. It's clear that, because of the pressure created by there being only one alternative, people's minds, even in a large-scale movement, are not open to a real and complete alternative. How could they be? It's no mystery: they can only be open if there is an active presence of militants in the movement – intellectuals, as a rule – who can represent and give impetus to the other alternative, even if it means splitting the movement. It's necessary to create and distribute flyers, organize discussions everywhere with everyone, take stock of the past with people, bring back certain aspects of the communist experience, arrange for the basic texts to be circulated, raise awareness of what happened during the Cultural Revolution, all that sort of thing. There need to be schools devoted to the communist hypothesis, "school" meaning that the communist hypothesis is discussed with everyone, that careful attention is paid to what people think, that the communist alternative is organized as broadly as possible, in keeping with the movement's intentions and the decisions that need to be made.

This is the same thing as Marx was trying to do, meaning that we're back at the beginning, that we have to start all over again. Fortunately, we know a little more than he did. We have to begin again, that is, we have to do our utmost to instill the idea of a different alternative and organize the struggle between these two alternatives in society. Later, the tactics to be adopted will be discussed. But we still need to put an end to the current impasse. That may be a long and difficult task, but it's a priority. The second point is that, armed with this, we need to deal with as many situations as can be dealt with; go where there are problems; connect with refugees, with people living in hostels, with workers in factories, with transient foreigners; go see what's happening in other countries; look closely at the new ideas that emerge whenever there are mass movements; and, on the basis of all these activist investigations, organize a debate between the two alternatives whenever possible. This is a feasible task. Actually, I think the situation was more difficult for Marx in 1850 than it is for us.

More difficult for Marx? What do you mean by that?

I've always been very interested in how long, difficult, extraordinarily severe the period of global reaction was after the revolutions of 1848. Because we talk about these revolutions, but what we forget is that they failed everywhere, without exception, and that they led to a protracted period of construction of a new kind of political reaction, either in an overtly bourgeois form or in the form of political innovations, as was the case with the Second Empire in France. Bear in mind that the upshot of the 1848 revolutions, in France, was the Second Empire! And in Germany it was Bismarkianism, and so on. So, all over Europe, either the consolidation of reactionary governments or the no less reactionary figure of aggressive nationalism took hold. And the counter-revolution was extremely vigorous in Russia, too.

Who are we talking about when we talk about Marx? No doubt the rather romantic Marx of the 1848 revolutions, in which he took part, with his rifle on the barricades. He was still young at the time. And then we talk about the Marx who played a role in the creation of German social democracy in the 1880s. But between the two, what did Marx do? What did he do for thirty years? He sat down at his desk and wrote *Capital*, while trying to create an International under very difficult conditions. The second bombshell, after the failure of the 1848 revolutions, was the crushing of the Paris Commune in 1871, which again reduced the worker movement, particularly in France, to a state of great weakness. So, when I say that this was a situation somewhat comparable to our own. . . . It could be said that the movements of the 1960s ultimately failed completely, that the "Arab Spring" uprisings of recent years also failed, just as the revolutions of the 1840s had failed. These failures nevertheless led to the emergence of a certain number of keepers of the flame (of whom I'm one of the survivors), who have worked actively and are paving the way for the advent of the third stage I was talking about, the new communism.

Essentially, the international and organizational situation faced by Marx and Engels in the 1850s was, I maintain, hardly any better than ours. One striking proof of this is that, around

1850 or 1860, nobody, apart from a tight little circle of activists, had heard of Marx yet. One of the examples I always use is Victor Hugo. Victor Hugo knew just about everything about everything. But Marx's name is nowhere to be found in his work. He may not even have been aware of Marx's existence! A retrospective Marx was therefore constructed, as though he'd been a great public figure of the nineteenth century. That was not at all the case. He was totally obscure, as, for that matter, was Lenin for a long time. No one among the European progressive intelligentsia had heard of Lenin before 1917, even though he had already written *What Is to Be Done?* in 1902, which later became a particularly famous work.

We need to remember all this: the career of revolutionary figures is often subterranean and has already gone through long periods of obscurity in the past. Long periods of obscurity that coincide every time, it must be said, with a boost in capitalism's globalism. Every time a further step in the expansion of globalization is taken, capitalism gains a lead over the communist alternative. This allows it to have new spaces and new adherents and to conquer new territories. Napoleon III in France was a combination of political authoritarianism, social liberalism, and all-out globalization. Kind of like Macron today.

Because how did Napoleon III get elected? Everyone has forgotten this, but he got elected on the promise of a return to universal suffrage. In the same way, today, Macron got elected on the promise of democratic totalization. He presented himself as the man who could reunite the country, since he was on both the right and the left. And then what did he do? He said: "I'm obviously maintaining the electoral system, democracy, but there will be an 'official candidate,' and it will be me . . ." This was the first time since Napoleon III that France has had an "official candidate,"[3] that is, a candidate who isn't the candidate of a party but, on the contrary, a party, hastily cobbled together, that is the party of a candidate, named Emmanuel Macron. The party's name is "La République en marche" [The Republic on the Move]. It could be called anything. In reality, it's Macron's party; it should be called "Macron

3 Under Napoleon III, the elections for the legislative body were between an official candidate, backed by the entire government apparatus, and an opponent who only acted as an opponent of the government.

on the Move," or MoM. Everyone knows that Macron and his inner circle tested and vetted, man by man and woman by woman, who their candidates in the various electoral districts would be. That's so typical of him. Let's summarize Macron's maxims: "I'm not on the right or the left; I'm sociable, I like everyone a lot; and I hold free elections, but you still ought to know which candidate I prefer. The least your president can do is tell you which candidate he prefers!" Like Napoléon III, Macron instituted the "official candidate."

What did Napoleon III do once he was in power? He signed the first free-trade agreement with England; he inscribed France in the globalization of the time, because signing a free-trade agreement with England was tantamount to integrating France into the capitalist system of the time. And that is indeed what's being asked of Macron by his CAC 40 cronies: to globalize, to unite, and at the same time to recommend in an authoritarian way who should be part of the executive staff, who is "qualified" for that: this is a figure that already appeared in France nearly two centuries ago. Something today reminds me of those times. Those times when, precisely, after the huge movements of the 1840s, after an initial revival of the communist idea, which had been seriously damaged as a result of a number of massacres in the streets of Paris, the bourgeois reaction had invented appropriate political structures, taking yet another step ahead in the development of globalized capitalism. That's what Macron is trying to do in France today.

And the worst thing is that the bourgeois bloc on both the right and the left agreed on the essentials – on the economic policies to be pursued, of course, but also on the issues of identity and security, basically – and so they're uniting . . .

It's fascinating. Macron is the bill come due from the previous decades, which has made it possible to get rid of the old political personnel who'd had their day and done their work. When Napoleon III came to power, too, there were absolutely odious local chieftains from the farthest provinces. Guys like Fillon [prime minister, 2007–12, and center-right candidate for president in 2017], so reactionary that they ended up hurting the cause. Well, under Macron, they've been able to get rid of guys like that. Macron's ascension made it possible to dump both Fillon and Madame Le

Pen [head of the far-right National Front Party, now known as the National Rally Party]. They were too old! They were too high-profile, they were causing problems. Capitalist leaders are very alert to any new developments. The enemy, so far, has always been a lot more sensitive to the slightest sign of change than we have been. For example, we really didn't see the political reaction of the 1980s coming. It had been covered up by Mitterrand until 1983. But *they* see things coming, and in 2017 they thought the time had come to draw the political conclusion from all this, namely to let a strong state entity work hand-in-hand with the real leaders of society, the big capitalists and high finance, the planetary oligarchy. This is the culmination of a perfectly logical process.

In a recent collection of essays, Un Parcours grec *(translated by David Broder as* Greece and the Reinvention of Politics, *Verso, 2018), in which you consider what we've learned from the collapse of the left represented by Syriza in Greece, after the hopes that had been raised in 2015, you stress the fact that what initially holds the public squares movements together, and subsequently makes them fail, is the strictly negative character of their demands. Could you elaborate on this problem, which we always ultimately come up against in today's world?*

We're back to the problem of the existence of the two alternatives, on the basis of which the possibility of politics arises. We can't be satisfied with the negation of one of these alternatives. Saying "Mubarak, get out" in Egypt is necessary but not sufficient. Mass movements are readily negative in that sense. People come together easily *against* something, but this being against something is not yet a politics. In this regard, the "against something" is rebellion. I would say once again with Mao Zedong: "It is right to rebel," and, indeed, if people *don't* rebel nothing ultimately happens. But rebellion doesn't immediately open a debate between the two alternatives. It amounts to saying that we don't want a particular aspect of the dominant alternative. Maybe we want something else, but that something else is still unclear. As I said, movements generally have a strong negative unity, but if people really discuss *politics* in a movement, it will inevitably divide. Why? Because the two alternatives exist in everyone's mind. It's a debate, a choice, an option. It's not the same as saying that this government is bad, and we don't want it.

It's absolutely necessary to take part in big mass movements and try to establish a *political* subjectivity within the *historical* uprising. This involves *putting something affirmative, something positive, on the agenda, the discussion of which will prove to be a special case of the struggle between the two alternatives*. It's not easy, because there is much more likely to be unanimous agreement about negation than about affirmation, but there's no way around it. If you think the unity of the movement is the single most important thing, the thing that must be preserved at all costs, then you'll fail because you won't be able to get the affirmative project to prevail over the easy negative unanimity. So, you've got to have the courage to say: "I'm part of the movement, but I'm also in favor of this particular hypothesis, this particular strategic path, and I'd like to know how the movement, in terms of the particular decisions it makes, connects with that orientation." It's necessary once again to adhere to a principle the Chinese introduced as a fundamental point of philosophical discussion. They asked: "Is the dialectic 'two that combine into one' or is it 'one that divides into two'?" They decided that the latter was the only true political principle.

Of the key political issues of our times, you have often said that the most important one today is what you call the "nomadic proletariat," the immigrant workforce carried along by deplorable globalization. You seem to think that that's the basis – what to do about it – for the current divide between reactive (or reactionary, if you prefer) politics and emancipatory politics. Could you clarify that idea?

If you look at all of recent history – the past fifty years in the West, let's say – it's absolutely obvious that a key issue, first, has been the formation of an international proletariat in every country. People speak about "refugees" now, but let's not forget that millions of foreign workers came to French factories beginning in the 1950s. There were Portuguese and Algerians, followed by Africans, and so on. I, who spent some time in factories, saw them, talked with them, socialized with them and was involved in politics with them. Already at that time, if you considered the proletariat in its most classic sense, that is, the mass of workers in the large factories, well, it was an *international* mass. That was already a very remarkable aspect, and it was possible to speak, as we did, of the "international proletariat of France."

Subsequently, from the 1980s onward, there was a process of massive deindustrialization in our country. So, we need to see things on a global scale. As I said just now, there are millions and potentially billions of people who are downright destitute, and the conditions for survival in their own countries do not exist. What do these people do? They leave. And, incidentally, given current conditions, they are undoubtedly right to do so. For someone on the verge of starvation, who has a family, to venture out in search of a place to live and support their loved ones, well, that's the least they can do, and it would be criminally absurd to hold it against them. People like this are what I call the "nomadic proletariat." On the one hand, this proletariat consists of the same sort of thing that has always existed, namely people who go to work on a regular basis in foreign countries; and, on the other hand, there is an ever-shifting mass of people fleeing substandard living conditions, either because the economic foundations of their lives have been destroyed because, typically, their lands, the little plots of farmland on which they eked out a living, were acquired by predatory consortiums and they can no longer work on them, or quite simply because there are terrible civil wars, religious wars, imperialist interventions by Western powers, and their countries have been devastated. So, I think that's essentially what the proletariat is today; it is this enormous mass of people roaming the surface of the earth, who, by virtue of their concrete situation, instantiate Marx's famous statement: "The proletariat has no country." Indeed, that declaration has become their reality, purely and simply: they have no country, they are seeking one. I therefore contend: politics consists and will consist of the intellectuals who are politicized in the direction of the new communism forging a bond with this nomadic proletariat and trying to organize it, as far as possible, in a new political movement. The International won't be just a laboriously constructed organization of representatives of various countries but something directly relevant to the global situation of these people.

Personally, I think meetings are the heart and soul of politics. Meetings are the heart of politics because – regardless of their size – they are where people affirm their existence and their capabilities. So, naturally you'll hear: "Oh, but getting all these people from around the world together won't be easy." But that's an objection for the sake of objection. Actually, a network of meetings, of gatherings, can easily be organized, a network that's effective in terms of analysis and decision-making, with regard to situations with global implications. Because it's important to bear in mind that capitalism, for its part, is entirely globalized today. The people running the large companies created by capital concentration are equally at home in Shanghai, Chicago, and Buenos Aires. The other alternative, the communist alternative, is lagging way behind that level of globalization. It is still largely trapped in a very narrow vision, in woefully national parameters. For example, I think the idea that our most urgent task is to pull out of Europe is very unconvincing. I think that, ultimately, if it degenerates into nationalist isolationism, there will always be someone more "nationally isolationist" than we are. Marine Le Pen and her clique are there to take care of nationalist isolationism.

Since the opponent's space is globalized, ours should be, too, and the various forms of nationalist isolationism are among the causes of the failure of the previous communist systems. In the final analysis, they failed to really internationalize, in that they said things like "We are the homeland of socialism." Actually, the "homeland of socialism" is somewhat at odds with the fact that proletarians have no country or homeland. Genuine internationalism is necessary. To that end, what *we* can do is meet extensively with people from all over the world, share in their experiences and take positions on a wide range of situations. What would probably be very useful today would be to found a world communist journal with an editorial board that would itself be globally diverse, that would be published in as many languages as possible and would consist of two things: theoretical, ideological, and political studies of the situation in the world, the construction of the other alternative today; and, in addition, reports on experiences of grassroots action, successes and victories achieved in one place or another, protests and mass movements. *That's* a project on the scale of the contemporary world – the project of the new communism.

You say not only that the issue of the nomadic proletariat is the *crucial political issue today, but that it is also the focal point for building a truly internationalist future politics. Let's zero in for a moment on that point, because the fact is, it would be a unique example of the politicization of enormous, completely cross-border groups, without there being a common language most of the time and without there being common organizations either, as there were, at one time, with the communist parties. Could you elaborate on the role you see this proletariat playing and the concrete ways of politicizing and especially of uniting it?*

When I say that this proletariat is "nomadic," it means, in particular, that there are fragments, elements, of this proletariat all over, including in the developed metropolises. It is obvious that, today, as has been the case for decades already, the very composition of what can be called the proletariat in France is in fact intrinsically international, meaning that it is characterized by many different languages, places of origin, customs, and religions. As I mentioned, the Maoist organization I belonged to had already in the 1970s proposed the concept of *the international proletariat of France*. It was a sort of shorthand, and it was completely justified because there was no getting around the fact that whenever we went into a large French factory we were immediately faced with the absolute necessity of talking to people who had either just arrived, or were about to leave, or were from foreign countries, people who were still illiterate for the most part, many of them not yet able to speak French. And it was one of the great failings of the PCF [the French Communist Party] and the CGT [the largest labor union in France] not to have organized those people, to have rigidly clung to a nationalist perspective, which later degenerated into the well known affair of the Communist mayor of Ivry using a bulldozer to demolish immigrant hostels, and the "Let's produce in France" campaign.

In other words, I really think this issue is present, including in every form of nationalism. It's not exactly a matter of organizing the proletariat on an international scale – I'll come back to that question, to the meaning of "organizing" – but of understanding that, today, anywhere, the organization of the proletariat cannot be clearly and simply integrated into a national framework. Even in the United States, a large proportion of the proletarians now are Mexicans who speak Spanish. Similarly, a significant proportion of the German proletariat consists of Turks. And even in Asia, where more than half of the world's proletariat is located, there are already processes of internationalization occurring in the factories. When I was in Korea, I learned that a portion of the residents of the huge workers' housing developments there came from Bangladesh. So, it's an absolutely global problem. There is an internal internationalism of the proletariat that is the result of its nomadism, of the fact that a great many people are forced to move around to find work as laborers anywhere today. In fact, the supply of potentially proletarian masses has dried up in the developed countries. The peasantry has been practically wiped out, and no one knows where to get new workers. They are eventually found, but they are from farther and farther away.

So, firstly, the nomadic proletariat should be considered not only as being a kind of global wandering mass – which also exists – that would have to be organized, with all the problems that you rightly point out, but also as figures of proletarian presence in the different countries, the developed countries included, and whose places of origin may be very far away. We see this here, where we're dealing not only with people from the former French colonial territories, the Algerians having arrived first, followed by the

Moroccans and then the Malians, and so on; but also, now, with people from even farther away: Tamils, people from the Middle East fleeing the turmoil going on there, people who are called refugees, Afghans, and so on.

So, the problem this poses is effectively one of organization, in new terms. We shouldn't forget that the idea that the organization of the communist movement had to be international in nature was a very early idea. Marx himself immediately focused on building such an International. He didn't focus primarily on building a German or English party. He immediately saw that internationalism was the only right approach for the development of the new alternative, the communist hypothesis. This is something that began, after all, with the first waves of immigration in the large French factories, with Italians or Poles even before the last war and then people coming massively from the African continent as early as 1950–60. It's not something new. I myself did that kind of political work for years among the objectively internationalized proletariat, along with my friends, first from the UCFml [Union of Marxist–Leninist Communists of France] and later from the Organisation politique [Political

Organization], and I can easily give an account of it. It involves special complications: meetings about the language acquisition process; schools that are ideological but also technical; protracted battles over the issue of worker stabilization, linked to the issue of identity documents, certificates of residence, and so on. Tons of problems that can have solutions if they're construed as problems from a militant perspective. And, in addition, this mass work attempts to bring into existence, in connection with the new communism, an international intellectuality that will gradually become part of local experiences. It's admittedly a huge agenda but a feasible one, and there have been some impressive grassroots experiments with it.

For the time being, it doesn't even exist in embryonic form, it's still non-existent . . .

For the moment, that's right, we're at an all-time low. For the moment, we're just barely at the stage of the ideological struggle for the *possibility* of this undertaking. We've been paying the price for the intellectuals' renegacy since the late 1970s. There were, and still are – a tradition going back to the Surrealists, via Debord – the stylish critical provocations and battles, as symbolic as they are courageous, of a certain ultra-left marked with melancholy, represented in France in recent years by the Invisible Committee.[4] However, the massive renegacy of the 1980s and 1990s was the intellectual expression of an equally massive show of support by people in the West for their beloved "democracy." Which means their support for liberal capitalism, terrified as they are by the global pressure of the nomadic proletariat. This identity-related tension over petty-bourgeois privileges in our society is not going to disappear overnight! That's why I often say that, from a historical perspective, we ought to repeat the 1840s or thereabouts — that is to say, the time when the task is to re-instill the idea that a radical alternative to globalized capitalism is possible. One statistic stands out from all the rest: for the first time in history, people who are

4 The Invisible Committee is an anonymous radical leftist collective that has published several works, including *The Coming Revolution*, and is associated with the Tarnac Nine, a group of people who were arrested for allegedly sabotaging overhead electrical lines on the French national railway. On April 12, 2018, the group was found not guilty of the charges of sabotage, conspiracy, and rioting, the terrorism charges having been dropped much earlier.

either workers or are looking for blue-collar work make up half the world's population. That wasn't at all the case in Marx's day. So, once again, and at a global level, the objective conditions are somewhat better than they were when Marx laid the theoretical foundation for the very first political communism.

That's true, but the people who were affected by the introduction of the communist idea in that century were more culturally homogeneous than today. Today, there are really people from every background among the ones you mentioned, coming from tremendously different worldviews. Between Korean workers, French or Sudanese proletarians, and Libyan migrants, what kind of solidarity can one hope to create? Constructing a common political subject out of all these different peoples, some of whom may be very vulnerable and displaced, seems extremely complicated . . .

I don't think it's much more complicated than constructing one with American workers and Russian workers was in the nineteenth century! I honestly don't think it is. You're right to point out the shift from internal migration within Europe to trips involving longer distances, but at the same time we know very well that there is a lot more global homogeneity today than in the past. There are common references and practices, there are shared technologies that connect people to each other, there is the ubiquitous experience of living in big cities, and so on, whereas in the nineteenth century, when rural, religious roots were extremely deep and dominant, that wasn't the case. Even in France, if you take the nineteenth-century working class, politicized subjects were a very small minority. What they were dealing with – this was very clear during the Paris Commune – were rural masses who were very hard to mobilize. Indeed, in working-class circles, rural people were spoken of with prejudicial disdain. Today, I don't think the problems should be overestimated. We can take advantage of the capitalist juggernaut: there's actually real work that's been accomplished by capitalist globalization. That's its only upside. That's its one true positive quality. When it comes to this issue, I remain a Marxist. Capitalist globalization destroys a certain number of identity, religious, racial, and national barriers. That's why there's such a strong identitarian and religious backlash today in some regions of the world, such as the Middle East, some areas of Africa, or even some

Eastern European countries. It's because modern capitalism, in and of itself, threatens them, since it is in fact perfectly indifferent to the whole conservative stockpile of identities. In this sense, there are problems that are even easier to solve now than before. After all, everyone knows what a cell phone is today, even in the remotest corners of the world! That was simply not the case before. Everyone knows what money is. Everyone knows what all sorts of things are that have become commonplace thanks to the multi-local power of the global market. It's up to us to ensure that everyone knows what the new communist idea is, too.

So, do you think it's the lack of a global political alternative today that gives this sense of total dispersion, this impression of seeing masses of atomized, isolated people, with no way of defending themselves against the enormous forces of global capitalism?

I absolutely think so. Especially since I know from personal experience that when you go into hostels that are home to illiterate Malians, who have come straight from the heart of Africa, it is entirely possible to speak with them, even though it may take some time getting used to it. This is so quite simply because the strategic project of the meaning of speaking with them exists, even for them, and therefore most of these workers are soon very glad to have us come and speak with them.

In fact, right now, the big problem is an intellectual one, not a cultural or identity, one. The problem is that, right now, we're still in a period of crisis of the Idea. You could call it the crisis of state communism, or the collapse of the socialist states, if you want to be more precise. Yes, the collapse of the socialist states is our real problem. It led to the massive bourgeois counter-offensive that was launched in the 1980s, with one of its ideological epicenters being France. This is because France has produced the greatest number of anti-totalitarian intellectuals – actually diehard reactionaries – and made them available, so to speak, to the whole world. With Bernard-Henri Lévy, André Glucksmann, Jean-Claude Milner, and Jacques-Alain Miller, we have, unfortunately, been treated to a totally new intellectual figure: the triumphant turncoat. All these young men – back in the day, around 1970 – had dabbled in militant Maoism. I saw them throw cobblestones through the windows of American banks to show their support for the Vietnamese war of national liberation. I saw them stomp on a stage in a university auditorium and say that all these temples of bourgeois knowledge had to be burned down. I saw them run through the fields, with the CRS [riot police] on their tails, after they'd attempted to forcibly occupy the Renault factory in Flins. I heard them shout "Marx! Engels! Lenin–Stalin–Mao! Long live the revolution!" I heard them call me a "right-winger" because I'd expressed some reservations about their methods of activism, their symbolic violence, their fanaticism that was inappropriate to the circumstances, and all their media hype. And then, disappointed because they had nothing tangible to show for all of this, they adopted the politically expedient stance of people who have had the (according to them) empty and quasi-criminal experience of communist totalitarianism and can therefore advocate liberalism, parliamentary democracy, and human rights with some authority and call for the democratic intervention of the US Army and French paratroopers wherever there's trouble. And they wrote "philosophical" books with all this nauseating liberal pap. They were called the "new philosophers," for as long as it took (and that time has almost, finally, come) for them to show that they were neither new nor philosophers. You know this better than anyone, you who have courageously exposed the aberrations, absurdities, and mumbo jumbo of this philosophical clique, an unsavory French specialty.

Fortunately, these "philosophers" are no longer our best-selling exports!

You're right, they're not our best export products. Besides, they copied a lot from American intellectuals who'd been around for quite some time. American reactionism was highly organized, especially in terms of economic thought. Anti-communism had long been second nature in the American academy. Guys like Hayek were on the neo-liberal frontlines well before our "new philosophers," who could be broadly defined as "new anti-communists," while their "democratic" arsenal, directed against the Idea, had been forged in the United States as far back as the Cold War era. The BHL [Bernard-Henri Lévy]-type French mainly played the – ultimately very important – role of people who aim to do away with everything the revolutionary French intelligentsia stood for, in terms of its global appeal. After a while, the

Americans realized that, as far as revolution and the new communism in our country were concerned, it was all over, and this is now written about everywhere as "Whatever happened to the French intellectuals?" It's quite true that reactionary French intellectuals are like small-town buffoons: nobody cares about them. Everyone already has their own local product on hand.

One of the obstacles to the return of the communist hypothesis is a kind of revival, at the philosophical level, of a conservative view of human beings. Let me explain what I mean. For a whole tradition of thought that goes from Hobbes to people like Jean-Claude Milner today, politics is what makes peaceful coexistence among people possible, a coexistence that is by definition dangerous in these thinkers' eyes. Ultimately, in this conservative view, politics consists in preventing crimes from happening. It is based to some extent on the fear of the other, and that's perhaps one of the biggest intellectual obstacles today to the revival of politics of emancipation. In a communist and emancipatory tradition, what can you counter that with? And how, as opposed to them, would you define the task of politics?

Contemporary democratic capitalism is one of the biggest criminals in history, after all! You've got to see that. I fully understand why we have an ethics that bans mass crimes, but it's a joke to think that the West as it is today is best qualified to police such an ethics. If you want to count deaths, let's count them: let's count the deaths that are a direct result of the colonial imperialisms and their rivalries from 1850 to the present. You'll see that it's an unprecedented killing field.

Let me just give you one example. Ever since the Russian archives were opened in the 1990s we know that the total number of deaths in the Gulag during the Stalin years – about thirty years, give or take – was 1,400,000. That's a huge number, of course, and it requires explanation and assessment. But it's almost exactly the number of French deaths that occurred in four years, and among a much smaller population than the Soviet Union's, during World War I! And there was no reason for that inconceivable bloodletting other than the imperial rivalry between the Franco-British bloc, which had the monopoly on colonial mass crime, and Germany, which wanted to equal it. It was on account of that despicable issue, and without in any way resolving it (they had to begin all over again, in an even worse way, in 1939), that young peasants from every little village were wiped out by the hundreds of thousands in the appalling conditions of life in the trenches. I maintain – boldly, given the current context – that this one comparison does not favor the French fetish of "our Republic." Absolutely not.

I'd also like to point out how carelessly the statistics, when it's a question of "communist totalitarianisms," are handled, provided they represent "the right deaths," so to speak, the ones on the heaps of which anti-communist propaganda will be based. And this infects even great minds, even communists! In the 1970s Louis Althusser once spoke to me about the "twenty million victims of the Cultural Revolution." Yet today, even staunch foes of communist China, who can hardly be suspected of wanting to play down its violence, cautiously put forward the figure of 700,000 in ten years. That's a huge difference! And don't get me started on the congenial female TV host who, toward the end of a show, breezily asked me: "What about the two hundred million victims of communism?"! Propaganda like that, in its zeal, would end up wiping out all the people involved.

There *is* an issue of crimes, but in no way does

it lead to the conservative conclusion, i.e., blind praise for the Western "democracies" and their so-called "values." That's what I think. On the contrary, "republican" conservatism, today, is a political attitude that is probably paving the way for very serious crimes, because it will end in fierce competition among the economic actors of the day, which has always led to war. After all, in today's world, war is already looming. The situation in the Middle East is arguably very similar in some respects to the situation in the Balkans before World War I: an imbroglio involving destatified regions, armed gangs everywhere, all the great powers getting involved, sending in their aircraft, and so on. And then one fine day there will be an incident – it was the assassination in Sarajevo in 1914; it can be just about anything today – and it will set off a firestorm. Look at the situation in the South China Sea, for example, where everyone is vigorously rearming.

It is ridiculous to depict the current situation as one in which the "international community," that is, the consortium of dominant capitalist countries and their corrupt clients, is organizing, with scrupulously democratic ethics, the fight against mass massacres, massacres for which barbarians alone are responsible. I had a discussion about this issue (and this is only one example) with my friend Jean-Luc Nancy, concerning Libya. He argued that the French military intervention in Libya was justified, since a massacre was about to occur there, for certain, in Benghazi, a massacre intended and planned by Qaddafi. What is certain in any case is that, ever since the intervention, which was marked by the assassination of Qaddafi with the direct complicity of our troops, that country has been completely devastated, dismembered; massacres occur every day; armed gangs impose their grim rule everywhere; and the country has, as it were, disappeared, to be replaced by banditry of every sort. This is exactly what happened in Iraq after the American intervention.

So, the reality is that it's outrageous to call in international police forces against crimes when it's a known fact that these same police forces are themselves behind the greatest crimes. There is no question that, since the 1950s, what with wars and "humanitarian" operations, the "democratic" nations of the international community have killed, or created the opportunity for killing, more people than any other player on the world stage. How can we still call nations "democratic" that, without being accountable to anyone, assume rights of policing, destruction, and torture (yes, really!) all over the world? Countries where the heads of state, in the greatest secrecy, sign authorizations for the assassination of this or that individual, carried out at the cost of "collateral" damage, whereby ten completely innocent people are killed for the sake of one successful assassination? This barbaric practice clearly exists in France, and the innocent, peace-loving François Hollande used it even more than his predecessors did. Likewise, it is known that the calm, administrative, long-distance drone-targeted assassination was the kind of decision that the charming Obama very often made, regardless of the price that would be paid in "accidental" victims. Even the manner in which the retaking of the city of Mosul from the Islamic State by the "international coalition" was accomplished turned the observers' stomachs: the city was razed to the ground, there were countless civilian victims and hundreds of thousands of people made homeless.

If the desire is really for peace, it is certainly not in the currently dominant sole alternative, the "democratic" arrogance of Capital, that it will be found. What has emerged from this alternative are big sharks, big state monsters in the service of a revitalized capitalism, which is paving the way for a situation comparable to that of the late nineteenth century for us, when, with rivalries and power plays prevailing, major political pathologies appeared. Even now the crudest forms of nationalism are reappearing everywhere: we've got to deal with people like Trump in the United States, or like the leaders of Poland and Hungary, and with the renewed and very active ambitions of the newcomers, China and Russia, who are demanding a seat at the table, just as Germany did before World War I. We are by no means in a world where democratic conservatism guarantees anything for us.

If the purpose of politics is not to protect us from violence from one another, as this whole philosophical tradition thinks it is, then what is *its purpose?*

The basic aim of politics, in my opinion, is to ensure that humanity is seen to be capable of determining its own destiny, in a fundamentally peaceful, because egalitarian, configuration. To that end, politics must be free from an interest regime that, because the interests are private or, by extension, state, interests, is inherently competitive. And so, let's begin by ensuring that these incredibly dominant interest regimes, whose concentration continues unabated, are prevented from preying massively on the world. Let's show how a way of organizing society that is completely divorced from capitalism is really possible.

4

What Does "The Left" Mean Today?

While waiting for the hypothetical return of a large-scale communist politics, what should our attitude be toward the existing left-identified options? I'm asking you this because people feel a lot of confusion, a lot of weariness, when it comes to the policies imposed on them, and you can't respond to that simply by waving before them the prospect of a revolution in the next few hundred years. Quite simply because everyone only has one life, and in terms of that life, people would like to experience a few tangible political victories from time to time.

I understand that.

Sometimes – and this is the case with Jacques Rancière, too, whatever the differences between you – you can seem to be extremely critical of the existing political options, whether it's the Invisible Committee or La France insoumise [Unsubdued France],[5] *not to mention the public-squares movement that we were talking about earlier . . . As a result, many people feel very discouraged, and the anger aroused by the situation subsides. People don't know where to expend that political energy.*

I completely understand that concern. But you see, there's one ineradicable fact. If you go on believing that significant victories in politics can be won in the current context of domination, you'll never get anywhere. You'll never get anywhere because historical experience shows that only one thing is really required of you, which is to think that, on the whole, the existing order is the only one possible. You're not required to think it's good. You may even think it's bad. That's not a problem as long as you actually think, deep down, or indeed subconsciously: "OK, I'll go through the motions of protesting, but there's no alternative, so I need to get a good job in the real world." As a result, the issue of the other alternative is crucial, that's just the way it is. It's

5 La France insoumise is a left-wing populist and democratic socialist political party launched in 2016 by Jean-Luc Mélenchon.

crucial because it provides a different definition of what constitutes a political success, including a strictly local one.

Nowadays, to tell the truth, a political success is nothing much. The world order implies that it's just a small concession wrung from the real master. I'm not making light of that, quite the contrary, but I think that what will remain of this small concession will be judged in terms of whether or not it has strengthened the general belief in the possibility of another alternative and given that possibility a boost. As such, there may be what appear to be big concessions extracted from our masters that are ultimately worthless.

That was the case with the record of Mitterrandism, which we really need to examine. The implementation of the Common Program represented major concessions.[6] There was a re-nationalization of virtually all credit. There were nationalizations of several large conglomerates. It was a fantastic program, actually! Much more far-

6 The Common Program was an alliance of the Socialist Party, the Communist Party, and the centrist Radical Movement of the Left, which succeeded in bringing François Mitterrand to power in 1981.

reaching, for example, than the Popular Front's. But, ultimately, what did this victory amount to? It was a Pyrrhic victory, literally. It immediately preceded, by just a few short years, a reverse process, a very rapid process, which began with the liberalization of credit by a Socialist minister.

What's your take on this backtracking by Mitterrand?

From the time it was drafted in the late 1970s, the Common Program of the Socialist and Communist Parties was stuck in the impasse I'm describing. The leftmost idea behind the program (there were quite a few opportunists who didn't even believe in it) was something like this: We're going to change the system from within, with respect to a few important issues, and that way we'll have scored a crucial point for a later stage. The truth is, they hadn't in the least scored a crucial point, and, as for a later stage, after barely three years in power they went back to liberal dogmas. Because to score such a point, to the extent that it is possible, means imposing something that, in terms of its own development, conflicts explicitly and irrevocably with the established order in its current form. And, in order to do that, you have to work, intellectually, not within the established order that you're trying to subvert with respect to one issue or another, but within the struggle between the two alternatives that I've been talking about since the beginning of our conversation.

What is basically lacking at the present time are intellectuals. People say there are no workers anymore, and so on and so forth. But the workers are elsewhere; they're in China, for example, and overwhelmingly so. This is the first time, I repeat, that they account for 50 percent of the world's population. There *are* workers, even here there are. And some of them, as we know, overwhelmingly abstain from elections, or don't have the right to vote, or vote for the far right, because, in the absence of an active communist alternative, it's the only force that they perceive as being outside the dominant system. We must, and we can, win these workers back over to the new communist cause. It will require activists, and therefore also – especially when genuine politics begins again – intellectuals. But it's precisely they who are lacking. Because an indispensable condition for being an intellectual in politics today is being someone who is really involved with working-class issues, who is able to think and speak with elements of the international proletariat, and who, in so doing, is not afraid of the word "communism." These are absolute criteria. They really are, trust me. Here in particular, but actually all over the world, we've managed to establish the same relationship to the word "communism" as that of the worst Americans on the far right in the 1950s. In other words, it's become an unmentionable word.

Even the pale-pink Socialist Party candidate in the last French presidential election was called a communist so as to discredit him . . .

Of course! Knowing that it was a deadly label, which he would therefore have to defend himself against. That's of course a sign of the failure of twentieth-century state communism . . . But it's also a sign of considerable ideological and subjective revenge on the part of the principal adversary, which, knowing that it has succeeded in making that word unmentionable, may assume that the only mentionable thing in politics is its own existence, since its own existence has never been challenged except by communist-type revolutions, organizations, and intellectuality. If that word is unmentionable, then what does "Unsubdued

France" [La France insoumise, Mélenchon's party] mean? Unsubdued by what order? I recently read that even the Communist Party is thinking of changing its name now, as the wily, cunning, sly fox that the Italian Communist Party has been throughout its existence did long before it.

The Communist Party hasn't been communist for ages . . .

Changing its name won't be a great historical event, I agree with you. But it's nevertheless symptomatic of the prevailing parliamentary totalitarianism. Valls [Socialist prime minister, 2014–16] wanted to remove the word "socialist" from the Socialist Party's name. Pierre Laurent [head of the French Communist Party] wants to remove "communist" from the Communist Party. It's really sort of farcical, as you can see. The accursed nature of these words is symptomatic of the fact that, in reality, there is no longer any revolutionary intelligentsia, strictly speaking, today, and maybe even no really progressive intelligentsia.

Let's go back to what you were saying a moment ago: we lack intellectuals. Could you elaborate on that?

One very recognizable feature of genuinely revolutionary politics throughout its development has been the real, recognized, accepted relationship between intellectuals and a relatively large portion of the popular masses. That's a fundamental feature. It's almost physically recognizable. Take Robespierre, for example, not in the Assembly and the Convention but in the Jacobin Club. Likewise, consider Lenin in 1917 and the years following: he was an intellectual standing at the podium in enormous mass meetings of workers. What you see is a degree of immediate understanding and mutual involvement between people who are intellectuals, who have written major political texts and analyzed the situation, and popular masses who have understood something of that, with intermediaries who explain it, make it come alive, and so on. That's a sure sign that something politically important is happening. It has taken more than two centuries since then for there to be communist intellectuals. Yet, there's a tremendous dearth of them all over the world today, because the people who were particularly affected by "the desire for the West," by inclusion in the ideological reaction of the 1980s, were mainly the intellectuals. It wasn't the workers who were responsible for those people's success. It was the intellectual petty bourgeoisie who adored the "new philosopher" renegades I mentioned a little while ago, because they embodied the intellectual petty bourgeoisie's disavowal of the earlier period, the realization it had come to about the failure of state communisms, and so on. So, it's true that what's lacking, what's scarce, what's in short supply today is an intelligentsia. There has never been a great revolutionary leader who wasn't an intellectual! Even Stalin was forced to assume that identity. When asked who he was, he ended up saying: "I'm an intellectual."

Even when those kinds of revolutionary intellectuals exist today, establishing a connection with the working classes nevertheless remains a big challenge . . . The left still has a lot of work to do before it can reconnect with the people.

Look, if there were more of them and if they spoke more . . . I'm going to tell you something really anecdotal that might sound like bragging. I'm only mentioning it because it's really symptomatic. Almost every day I get stopped on the street by someone, someone who's not an intellectual, I assure you. And who more often than not is clearly from somewhere other than our part of the world. That man, or that woman, has not read my books. Some of them tell me how they found out about me. They saw me on Taddeï a few years ago[7], they saw me on TV or heard me on the radio, or someone gave them one of my interviews in this or that publication to read, they looked me up – and, yes, this is absolutely true – they very often listened to one or another of the "Contre-courant" programs the two of us do (one of which this book is based on)[8], where we give other intellectuals the opportunity to speak. And so they thank me. Really! There they are, and they say: "You're Alain Badiou, aren't you? Well, I'm glad I ran into you because I wanted to thank you."

That's really very telling. Actually, what's terrible is my isolation. What I mean, of course (so that I'm not instantly accused of being paranoid),

7 Frédéric Taddeï hosted a cultural show, "Ce soir ou jamais," on French TV from 2006 to 2016.

8 The "Contre-courant" programs in which Badiou and Lancelin interview and debate various intellectuals can be viewed on YouTube or at the website of the Théâtre de la Commune in Aubervilliers (http://lacommune-aubervilliers.fr/emission-contre-courant).

is "our" isolation, but it's still a very small group I'm talking about. That's the point. Honestly, isolation was not what I wanted. When someone perfectly ordinary in the metro says "Thank you" to me, it's very gratifying, but considering what I've been able to do, considering the present intellectual situation, it's also undeserved in many respects.

Marx, Engels, Lenin, the young Mao, and Trotsky, Rosa Luxemburg, and Castro were all intellectuals, of course. They started out by trying to organize, to gather together, enough intellectuals, like themselves, to speak in a controlled and intelligible way to other people, to rally ordinary people systemically, in a way that they could hear. Today, the arsenal the powers-that-be have at their command to prevent that type of speech from circulating amounts to a wall of considerable thickness. And that wall is intended to ensure that it doesn't happen, that it can't happen. The aim is to ensure at all costs that the minimal relationship between intellectuals convinced that other political scenarios are possible and ordinary people is ultimately very difficult to establish. Hence the considerable importance to the powers-that-be of having complete control over the media. By extension, anyone like you who gives the appearance of promoting such a connection has to be fired. They're afraid people will find out that something else is possible. They especially don't want it to be found out through their own media outlets. It's already too dangerous for them. Way too dangerous. In a way, they're right to be afraid because I can tell that that kind of speech has an immediate effect on ordinary people. They hear in it a tone they recognize as not being the typical one. It's not the self-addressed speech of an inner circle; it's addressed to them as well. It is clear enough, intelligible enough, simple enough for it to speak to them. That's the problem with the lack of intellectuals, you see. And changing that is a very long and difficult task.

You mention "ordinary people" and stress the importance of speaking in a way that can reach them again. That was precisely the task La France insoumise set itself in the last presidential election: to overcome the barrier that increasingly keeps the working classes at a remove from politics and to undertake a genuine work of popular education. You've said practically nothing about this: what do you think about this movement?

I haven't spoken about Mélenchon, and deliberately so. I'll tell you why. In no way do I want to be seen as someone who wants to undermine La France insoumise. I don't want to be put in that position. I can certainly understand why young people, workers, people from the Marseille suburbs, and so on voted for Mélenchon. I really can. In fact, that's what my own experience was like: when I was young, as I already mentioned to you, I was a leftwing social democrat. That's how I began, so I can't blame other people for starting out on their own political journey the same way I did! I repeat: since the nineteenth century all the intellectuals who eventually became revolutionary intellectuals began, more or less, in that leftwing social-democratic, or "moderate" communist, milieu. They were always involved in schisms in social democracy. Like Marx and Engels being highly critical of the German Social Democratic Party, like Lenin creating the Bolshevik faction, like Mao by the late 1920s opposing the majority of the Chinese party on crucial issues. A little like Mélenchon, after all, building his organization outside the Socialist Party . . . The reason I find Mélenchon hard to take and why I don't at all believe he's committed to the project of a different political alternative is his total defense of Mitterrand's legacy. Frankly, that's an awful model! If all it amounts to is a rehash of Mitterrand, well, thanks but no thanks! If, when he says, "We're ready to govern immediately," it's in reference to a model like that, then no, no way. But what I do hope is that, via Mélenchonism, people able to internalize the need and urgency for a new political alternative will start appearing, particularly among the educated youth. I don't think that Mélenchon, by himself and as a movement, is the vehicle for a genuine alternative, but that's not a crucial objection because it's in such opposition parties, even splinter parties, that young people can cut their political teeth, discuss things, meet other intellectuals, and so on. And that's great. Actually, it's an attempt to reconstruct leftwing social democracy, which has always been necessary for the emergence of a new version of communism. After all, with the *Critique of the Gotha Program,* our founding fathers, Engels and Marx, were also schismatics of German social democracy. And I myself, having been a schismatic of the SFIO, which is a lot worse, neither can nor want to throw stones at anyone. But nor is my role, my particular usefulness in the current situation, to give my unquestioning blessing to this type of parliamentary escapade. It's of no interest in terms of my own objectives, and I would be of no use in doing so.

In reality, the French parliamentary system has been thrown out of whack, fundamentally, by a gradual blurring of the difference between the parliamentary right and left. Basically, the systemic legitimacy of the existence of the right/left system, as the illusion of a real choice, disappeared with Hollande, after having taken a beating from Jospin [Socialist prime minister, 1997–2002], who had himself followed in the footsteps of the "second" Mitterrand. When there's this kind of de-legitimation of the right/left choice, the threats to the existing system build up on the extremes: on the far right, where a revanchist, identity-based, traditionalist current emerges – Trump or Le Pen – but also on the far left, where something might resurface. That's what happened in 2017, and the gang governing us overcame those threats by concocting their own "neither right nor left," or, let's say, their "right and left" catch-all system.

It all worked like a parliamentary coup

d'état because, instead of relying on one of the components of the parliamentary system, they manufactured one outside it. As a result, the traditional left and right are now discredited and powerless. This being the case, it is perfectly natural and logical that a new movement, or one regarded as new, should emerge within the parliamentary system, on its leftmost wing. And that's the role Mélenchon is playing right now. The political future is always linked, more or less, to this sort of adventure, even if things only become really serious when the adventure is itself shaped from within by contradictions and becomes more radical by being to some extent part of the struggle between the two alternatives and therefore related to the new communism.

5

Macron, or the Democratic Coup d'état

In what sense can we speak of a "democratic coup d'état," the phrase you used to describe the election of Emmanuel Macron in May 2017? Can you explain what was so special about that election, as compared with those of his predecessors? Because, after all, it could be said that François Hollande also belonged to that second, socialist right wing, and that, before him, Nicolas Sarkozy was already a sort of agent of the CAC 40 – remember the night at Fouquet's,[9] *among other exploits . . .*

9 Sarkozy, the so-called "bling-bling president," was criticized for celebrating his 2007 electoral victory at the glitzy Paris restaurant Fouquet's in the company of influential people from the worlds of business, the media, finance, and so on.

Yes, but I think that Macronism has to do, first and foremost, with traditional party politics in the parliamentary organization of our modern society, and that it subverts it in an authoritarian way. The way the modern parliamentary system of, let's say, the Western "democracies" works is that there are two government parties that alternate in power. In France, it was the left and the right; in Germany, social democracy and Christian democracy; and in America, the Democrats and the Republicans. It doesn't matter! In any case, the bottom line was the same in these different variations. What specifically happened, not just in France but everywhere, actually – the cases of the United Kingdom and the United States are telling, with the success of Trump's far right in the US and the still relative, yet highly symbolic, success of Corbyn in the UK, which is reactivating militant post-war Labourism – was a throwing into crisis of what the combining of the two government parties had become, for the past twenty or thirty years, actually, i.e., something increasingly indistinguishable. In the United States there was deep disillusionment with Obama's actual ability to achieve reform. And in France everyone saw that Hollande's "reforms" were nonexistent.

What happened is that this systemic crisis of the parliamentary system created the opportunity for what I in fact call a "coup d'état." What a coup d'état means is that things won't happen in and through the existing parties; they will emerge from the conjuncture itself. That's why it's a "coup," in the strict sense of the word [meaning "a blow"], that is, a coup that only the particular situation allows for, not the ordinary constitutional system, the entrenched habits, and so on. And it's a coup *d'état* because it's a coup that takes state power without going through the usual stages of creating a party that grows little by little, and so on. No, no, not this time! In a very short time an apparatus is set up that will take state power.

One of the characteristic features of this set-up is the fact that the party's power will come from the personalization of the state. What this means in actual fact is that a man who came to state power by whatever means (democratic ones in this case, since he was elected, after all) will build from scratch the party machine that supports him politically and constitutes his legitimacy. And he'll get it approved by a vote that, as it's a vote for him *personally* – what's more, without anyone really knowing who he is and what he really intends to do – is a fake parliamentary vote. In reality it's a plebiscite vote. The current National Assembly is the outcome of a plebiscite in favor of Macron. It's not the normal outcome of an "old-style" electoral contest. And, as a matter of fact, everyone is well aware that the party's platform was extremely vague. It wasn't overwhelming support for a specific platform that accounted for its success. No way! It was a man, a narrative . . . And a relentless hype campaign warning: "If he doesn't win, you're going to get the far right!" That played a decisive role.

Yes, of course. But also, unfortunately, from a political point of view, Macron and his followers managed to impose certain issues at the crucial time and to win certain cultural battles, even in some working-class neighborhoods, especially among a whole base of voters who are very afraid they'll never be able to enter the labor market. The idea that stripping away the labor market's protections could facilitate inclusion – that sort of specious reasoning, that totally misguided common sense – had a significant impact. There was rampant propaganda to that effect, which allowed him to pick up some votes beyond those of his core middle-class constituency . . .

I'm well aware that, as usual, those were false but effective promises. But, at the same time, they're linked to longstanding propaganda, dating from well before Macron, according to which France's problem is labor costs, on the one hand, and government handouts to the poor, on the other. The labor code, social security, and welfare recipients are allegedly the three evils plaguing the country. To go along with an agenda like that you already have to have a pretty twisted mind, I'm sure you'll agree! It's clear that it's directly related to the terrible lack of a real vision of what our society is, of who's in charge of it, of the global system it's part of, and so on. It always comes down to the extreme lack of any real alternative, of the (provisional) absence of any possibility of communism.

People have been deprived of the means to develop a political point of view in this country, as has long been the case in the United States. The media are controlled, the unions are powerless or have simply been destroyed or bought off, the left has been discredited for quite some time because of its unbelievable track record of compromise. Everything was ripe for the emergence of a Macron.

Exactly. At the same time, this combination of different factors – the emergence of someone who was unknown only a few months before, the absolute personalization of power, and the manufacturing of a totally artificial party out of this personalization of power – makes it possible for me to use the term "coup d'état" in a general and rather neutral, descriptive sense. The idea that a coup d'état is necessarily military and anti-democratic is a narrow definition of "coup d'état," because "coup d'état" and "military coup d'état" are thereby considered to be identical. If that were the case, even the coming to power of Hitler, who was lawfully appointed Chancellor by an assembly after a regular election, would not be a coup d'état. Nor would Pétain's coming to power in 1940, which was overwhelmingly supported by the National Assembly that was elected in 1936 – the Popular Front assembly, it should be noted.

De Gaulle, of course, came to power in 1958 through a coup d'état that, in this case, was largely military. It's all been covered up since then, but I know about it from personal experience. Paratrooper units were threatening the National Assembly. They had already seized power in Algeria, after all, and invaded Corsica. My father, who was the Socialist mayor of Toulouse at the time and implacably opposed to the Algerian War and the colonial army, set up an armed defense with his old Resistance buddies on the road between Toulouse and Pau, the base from which it was rumored that military units would move out. OK, well, there was nothing of the kind with Macron. But it was still a "coup," because it all developed on the basis of the take-over of the state, including the legislative elections that followed, which were actually a plebiscite referendum voting "yes" on Macron. And the idea that if they didn't back him, the alternative would be worse is also an organized reaction, typical of this kind of coup. "If we don't support good old Pétain we'll wind up with the Nazis . . . or the Communists." They always wave that kind of red flag. Take Marine Le Pen, for instance. She never had the slightest chance of being elected! No poll ever gave her more than 40 percent. It was a total joke. So, this coup was also based on false panic, fabricated largely by the compliant media and indoctrinated intellectuals, who were even more abject than usual this time around. I give the whole set-up a dialectical name: a democratic coup d'état. The appearances of democracy were respected, for the most part, but it was a coup d'état. That's why, when all is said and done, the only sensible people in this whole affair were the abstentionists. At least *they* didn't participate in this cruel farce.

One could go even further, insofar as there are clearly identifiable financial forces behind Macron that have been waiting to make their move, or plotting their coup, as it were, for several years now actually. Macron was a virtual unknown, a bit player, to the French, of course, but not to those backroom bosses, since, as Deputy Secretary General of the Élysée [in Hollande's first government] and then as Minister of the Economy [under the second Valls government] he was the hub of the whole CAC 40 at that level of power . . .

I agree with all that. If you want to describe "Macron's coup d'état" in terms of its class significance, you write what Marx wrote about Napoleon III in *The Class Struggles in France*, published in 1850; it was much the same thing. Because the legitimation of the coup d'état was ultimately, and in both cases, intended to allow for a complete and total takeover by the French capitalist caste that took the forms previously mentioned. Many so-called social-democratic intellectuals – I've run into some recently – refuse to believe that things happened that way. They think it was an inevitable modernization of French political life, which was in the grip of archaic forces. For many of these idiots, who also happen to be nefarious individuals, the "agent of capital" aspect of governments is not even a problem. They take it for granted that politicians may be lackeys of the oligarchy, telling themselves "That's the way it is today." But in fact, they're afraid that genuine politics might return, the politics that, with the struggle between the two alternatives being revived, would force them to say who they are exactly and not hide, under the pretext of democracy, behind the existing order's inevitabilities.

But is there any political advantage to be gained from what is ultimately a clarification of the situation? It's clear that, now, capital barely attempts to conceal itself and operates in broad daylight . . .

Well, that's what we shall see. Let me tell you what I think. The big deal behind all this is the fact that Macron wants to revise the status of civil servants in France. And that's a huge deal.

If he attempts that, he'll be breaking a taboo that dates almost back to Louis XIV. Ever since that time, civil servants have been the go-betweens between the state's authority and a significant portion of the population. Does he intend to do that? I think he does. His backers want him to. And Fillon's announcement that 500,000 jobs would be eliminated was just a trial balloon, a testing of the waters[10]. In any case, civil service status is a national peculiarity. That's very clear to me. My best former students from Germany are remarkable people who are always signing two-year assistant professor contracts in universities, and getting tenure there is very complicated. You only become tenured at the age of forty or fifty. The American, German, and English systems are systems that build job insecurity into the entire civil service. In the reckless glee of the oligarchy contemplating its pure product, Macron, in power, you already hear that "all public-sector jobs should be eliminated"! That would be the

10 As the center-right candidate for president in the 2017 election, François Fillon, who had been prime minister under Sarkozy, promised to slash 500,000 public-sector jobs in five years.

fulfilment of a distinctly anti-communist agenda: basically, eliminating everything that is common to us all, and handing our health, children's education, and public transportation over to global mafias. And a case could be made to the public that "there's no reason why these people should have jobs for life since nobody has that kind of guarantee, for life, or even, often, for a month, or indeed for a week." I think *that* would mean war.

The government is already preparing to convert certain CDIs [*contrats à durée indéterminée*, meaning indeterminate duration, or permanent, contracts] into so-called "project" contracts that will offer less protection than the current CDDs [*contrats à durée déterminée*, meaning determinate duration, or temporary, contracts]. This is extraordinary. Linguistically, it fascinated me: that the word "indeterminate" can mean "strictly determinate." A project contract is indeterminate, except that it's only for the time it takes for the project to be completed. That's extraordinary! The reactionary forces' verbal inventions are always amazing. This project contract is a literally Hegelian, profound dialectic because we're being told that the essence of the indeterminate is the determinate in the strictest sense of the word: it's determined by what we do, i.e., a project. So, it's an indeterminate contract, provided that the indeterminacy is simply an actual, measurable determinacy! I thought that was wonderful.

Here's where we see how important it is to control all the media, because this whole thing can actually be very easily discredited. Yet it will only be so to a limited extent.

Well, *I* in any case will discredit it every chance I get. We've got to tell people all this, explain how important it is to be wary of language! When a word, CDI, is retained, you've got to see the price that's paid for retaining it, namely its pure and simple negation. It's a CDID, a contract with a determinate indeterminate duration.

The two problems, the two very important issues, are therefore the CDI and civil service status. I don't know whether the reforms will pass. We'll see. It doesn't depend on us, it depends on historical eventuality, on the degree of public awareness; it depends on circumstances, really. What we can do, if there really is a "we" – which is a huge problem – is campaign wherever we can on the gravity of this kind of issue, which is actually the revenge of the so-called "upstanding citizens" against the people. Revenge for all the progressive events in the history of France, from the right-to-strike laws in the late nineteenth century to the verifiable contractualization of labor rules beginning with the Popular Front, to the achievements of the National Council of the Resistance after the war.

There is a ferociousness to the bourgeoisie when it feels free. They want to get rid of everything, they really do. And they use Germany as an example. In France, the reactionaries have always followed Germany's example. Yet, I repeat, 30 per cent of the population there is in severe poverty. It's important to be aware of that. Germany has massive, American-style poverty. Do people here, ordinary people, realize that that's what they're being led to? That that's what they're being dragged toward? Apparently, they don't realize it at all, even though that's what Macron's buddies want: they think there needs to be a much larger tier of poor people than is presently the case. This is because the French bourgeoisie is absolutely convinced that its weak position in the global market is linked to inflated labor costs and overly strong work contract protection. The millionaires' mafia sees dangerous people with privileges everywhere! The gutting currently underway is going to lead to a significant increase in profits for the biggest corporations and create a no less significant mass of severely impoverished people, not to mention a huge expansion of the private sector. The ultimate ideal of capitalism is for the air we breathe to be privatized and lead to worldwide financial trafficking – never forget that. For now, we can foresee the increasing privatization of public education, which is already rampant. And the privatization of the hospital system, which is already at a very advanced stage.

And in the meantime, that same hospital sector that was until recently the pride of France will become poorer, with people failing to make the connection between this phenomenon and the already enormous government handouts that were given to companies during the previous five-year presidential term.

We need to wage a real campaign on the systemic, capitalistic link between each of these issues. And use it as an opportunity to explain clearly, with these examples, what can and must be the alternative: the new communism. We also need to stress that the people who will be reduced to overwhelming poverty will also be people who will have trouble affording medical services, even essential ones, and who will be offered only bottom-of-the-barrel schools. All of this is the truth, the reality, of Macron. So, he needs to be attacked right away; we shouldn't wait even one minute. I'm not very optimistic. We're really in a bad way. But we've still got to make sure that some of these measures are seen as truly outrageous and that they spark popular movements. That would be a point of protest from which to reopen the debate on the two alternatives. In a way, Macron can expose a dependence on contemporary capitalism that the traditional "left" concealed, since it claimed that we could do the right thing by remaining within the established order. Macron can be what the Chinese called "a teacher by negative example."

Conclusion

Regarding the obstacles to the return of a genuine political alternative that you're calling for, I'd like us to return one last time in this discussion to historical communism, to the extremely bloody image of it that people have in their minds, an image that grew out of the failures of the past century. Until this issue is resolved in people's minds, nothing can happen. What other, completely different form could communism take today?

Regarding the first point, I think first and foremost that we need to appreciate the fact, as I did at a recent conference on the Russian Revolution at the Quai Branly Museum, that the term "communism" – and to an even greater extent "communist revolution" – can only mean something that, because of its magnitude, its destiny, and so on, can only really be compared with the Neolithic Revolution. Communism isn't what Marx may imply at times. It's not a short-term solution resulting from the unfettered development of capitalism. It is actually a figure of the existence of humanity as a whole, one that breaks with a state of affairs that has lasted for thousands of years, namely inegalitarian societies, with the dominant group defined by its private ownership of the means of production and protected by a state. Macron, in this respect, is a perfect Neolithic man. So, the failure of the state communisms of the twentieth century should be judged against the fact that the communist idea, its historicity, and its development involve a long-term project. It's not something that today's capitalism is gearing up for imminently. That's why I completely disagree with the Invisible Committee and other sectors of militant ultra-leftism, whose analyses foster the illusion that the collapse of capitalism and the political domination it supports is a tactical and, what's more, an impending, issue.

My own conviction, based on facts, is that the communist overthrow of capitalism is not at all a tactical issue, let alone an impending one. The idea that with just a little push the global capitalist oligarchy will come crashing down strikes me as ridiculous. And I agree even less with those who think that capitalism is already dead and is going to crumble into dust any moment now. When the Invisible Committee thinks it's making history by taking over peaceful union demonstrations via militant commandos, it is reflecting the "let's push harder and it will all collapse" mentality. And when they see that nothing has ultimately happened, except for the fact that, with Macron, Capital has the upper hand more than ever, the Committee heads back to the countryside and becomes invisible again. I've received some articles written by young scholars explaining that, since capitalism is on its last legs, all we have to do is step aside and not participate for the capitalist machine, left all alone, to grind to a screeching halt. In New York, in front of a room packed with young people, I argued against a group of guys who think that, thanks to technology, work will be done by robots and all we'll need to do is give everyone a "universal basic income" for the world to be re-enchanted. To say that the end of work is on the cards right now, when about two billion people are willing to risk their lives in dilapidated boats to look for work in Europe or elsewhere, well, that's a bit much!

The truth is that capitalism is booming. It is actively dominating the whole of Asia, and eventually all of Africa, which is for the time being an imperial looting zone, will enter the regulated global game of production and exchange. We're at the very beginning of a very long process. So, there's nothing especially surprising about the fact that the very first attempts at communism, in Russia and China, which experimented from scratch with a type of post-Neolithic society, breaking with thousands of years of history, ended in failure. They conceived of themselves in terms of the idea of a rapid, even total, success, which was the idea of the official Marxism of the day. An instant success that made the category of revolution the basic category, without realizing that the category of revolution can only be an evental category, a rupture that leads to much bigger problems than the ones it resolves.

You tear down one form of government and replace it with another, but that doesn't mean that society has been changed. Everything will be judged by the way you change the social world, both objectively and subjectively, over the long term, with the four principles of communism I mentioned earlier as the criterion. In this regard, there is a revolutionary tacticism that's still very much alive and is due to the fact that people like victories, as you pointed out a little while ago. But actually, the idea of victory must itself be changed. That's why I'm inclined to think there are more victories than people imagine. Given the extraordinary difficulty of the process, a very localized victory – for example, the actual success of a meeting between three intellectuals and ten workers, who agree on a slogan appropriate to the local situation and on the communist nature, in the broad sense, of that slogan – should be regarded as a victory, perhaps even more so, in a way, than a fleeting electoral victory should be. So, the idea of victory needs to be revisited. In that regard, there was a sham notion of revolutionary victory in both the Soviet Union and China. It was long based on the model of swift victories and instantaneous changes, radical and irreversible ruptures, whereas that's not what it was about at all.

A new analysis of episodes – whether of defeat, such as the Paris Commune, or apparent victory, such as in the Soviet Union – should be done on the basis of this reassessment of the meaning of victory and defeat in the context of the communist idea. And that is a task that has by no means been completely accomplished. There were victories that haven't been celebrated as they should have been and defeats that have been mistaken for victories. This especially struck me, even when considering something as distinctive as the Cuban revolution. It was celebrated as the victory of an armed revolt in one place when in fact, on closer inspection, there was actually a very significant transformation of peasant life and social relations in general on the island, which was far more promising for the future than the guerilla army's military victory seemed to be. We should also remember that Mao, for his part, always had a very long-range vision. He always said that the question of which one – imperialism or communism – victory should ultimately be attributed to was a long-range question and that the answer would remain undecided for a very long time. This also explains his surprising statement, considering the complexity and apparent strangeness of the Cultural Revolution in China, that another seven or ten such revolutions might be needed to see things clearly.

The utmost consideration should also be given to the fact that the basic principles of communism cannot be reduced to the mere abolition of private property. Earlier, I spoke about the four principles of communism, and the question of property or ownership is only the first of the four. Of course, communism involves the elimination of the private ownership of the means of production and exchange. Fine. Both the Soviets and the Chinese achieved that. But it by no means prevented their ultimate failure.

In the final analysis, the two revolutionary ventures of the past century should be regarded not as a last-chance court for the communist idea but as a rough, insufficient start but a start nonetheless. An insufficient start, ultimately doomed to failure as far as its own principles were concerned, but such failures are not ends when it comes to the communist idea; they're beginnings.

If the failure was spectacular and, with the help of capitalist propaganda, often regarded as a definitive one, it is because it had been presented as a definitive success. Someone like Stalin, for example, could say: "The revolution is over." Part of the excitement stirred up by the Soviet experiment stemmed, moreover, from the belief that it was an irreversible, definitive success when in fact, from a historical perspective, it was a very interesting start, of course, but a shaky one and limited with respect to a number of basic issues. It is subjectively very important to put the failure in its proper perspective by showing that a large part of the responsibility for the failure came from a lopsided, unilateral understanding of what an actual, irreversible victory of the communist idea was.

But in the end, does everything we've talked about so far, all these problems and obstacles we've mentioned, amount to praise for politics? I'd like to ask you, by way of conclusion, whether politics can make people happy and what a really successful communist future would be like.

First of all, yes, absolutely, it *is* praise! Of all the endeavors – artistic, scientific, amorous, or political – of which humanity has shown itself capable, communism is without a doubt the most ambitious, the most comprehensive, and the one that will lift humanity dramatically above the laws of competition, of survival at any cost, of private interest, of constant hostile suspicion toward others, all of which are laws of brute life, laws of the animal world, laws of nature. The new communism, which includes a critical assessment of the earlier attempts without denying their importance and novelty, is, on the scale of society as a whole, the way out, at long last, of the Neolithic Age of humanity. It is absolutely worthwhile to identify with this perspective, even if it is on only one issue, in only one circumstance, knowing that what we're doing is both necessary and an absolutely free choice. We sense, we know, right away, that that is the true life. You asked me about happiness. Well, yes: the extraordinary difficulty of communist work is also the source of the most extraordinary happiness. I'm not talking here about a collective paradise where humanity would laze around as if it had rediscovered the tranquil joys of Adamic nakedness. No. What I'm saying is that whenever you and your companions in a political venture, faced with a very specific decision, thought, or action, know that you're *also* in an element of universality, and thus in virtual communication with all of humanity, then, as Spinoza says, you "know from experience that you are eternal."

Because every truth – be it the truth of a theorem that has finally been understood or that of a successful and promising political meeting – is an eternal work, of an eternity whose affect is a shared kind of bliss.